*TRAVEL ARIZONA*

# The Scenic Byways

*TWENTY-TWO FAMILY TOURS BASED ON OFFICIAL SCENIC DRIVES*

**TEXT**
PAULA SEARCY

**PHOTOGRAPHS**
*ARIZONA HIGHWAYS* CONTRIBUTORS

**PHOTOGRAPHY EDITOR**
PETER ENSENBERGER

**DESIGN AND ILLUSTRATION**
VICKY SNOW

**MAPS**
KEVIN J. KIBSEY

**COPY EDITORS**
EVELYN HOWELL AND LAURA A. LAWRIE

**BOOK EDITOR**
BOB ALBANO

## ARIZONA HIGHWAYS
### BOOKS

*Produced in cooperation with
the Arizona Department of Transportation's
Roadside Development Services
and the Federal Highway Administration.*

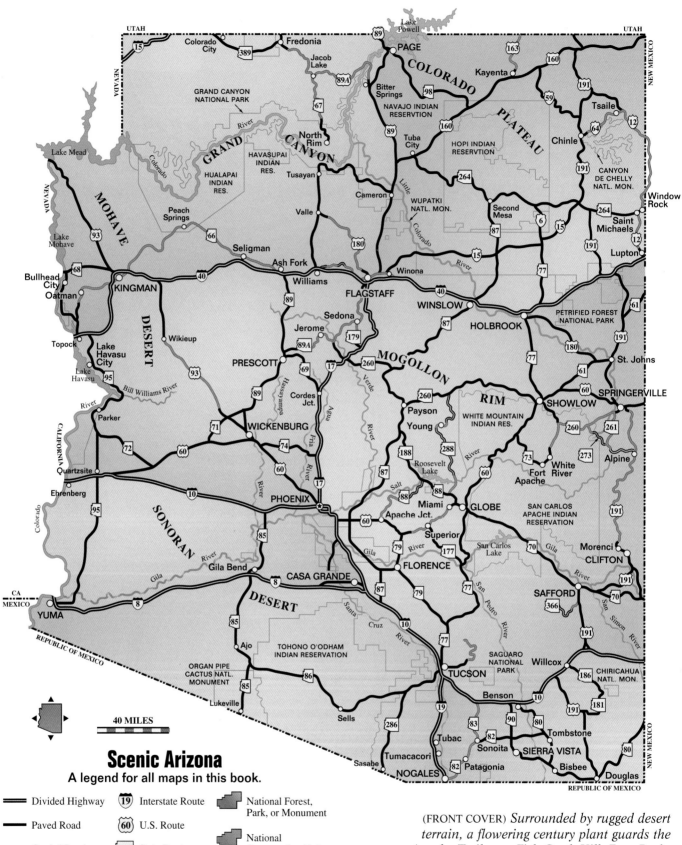

# Scenic Arizona
### A legend for all maps in this book.

| | |
|---|---|
| ══════ Divided Highway | 🛡19 Interstate Route |
| ━━━━━ Paved Road | ◯60 U.S. Route |
| ───── Graded Road | ▢260 State Route |
| ┅┅┅┅ Unimproved Road | ◯70 Indian Route |
| ━━━━━ Paved Scenic or Historic Road | ◯ City or Town |
| ━━━━━ Graded Scenic or Historic Road | △ Campground |
| | ▢ Place of Interest |

| |
|---|
| National Forest, Park, or Monument |
| National Conservation Unit |
| Indian Reservation |
| Wilderness Area |
| 〰 Perennial Stream |
| 〰 Intermittent Stream |

(FRONT COVER) *Surrounded by rugged desert terrain, a flowering century plant guards the Apache Trail near Fish Creek Hill. Four Peaks spreads across the horizon.* JERRY SIEVE
(INSIDE FRONT COVER) *Historic Route 66 crosses a flat expanse west of Seligman.* DAVID ELMS JR.
(BACK COVER) *Clearing storm clouds at sunset accent Mount Lemmon Highway, the route of the Sky Island Scenic Byway.* EDWARD McCAIN

*TRAVEL ARIZONA*
# The Scenic Byways

**CONTENTS**

Published by the Book Division of *Arizona Highways* magazine, a monthly publication of the Arizona Department of Transportation, 2039 West Lewis Avenue, Phoenix, Arizona 85009.   Telephone: (602) 712-2200   Website: www.arizonahighways.com

Win Holden — Publisher          Bob Albano — Managing Editor          Evelyn Howell — Associate Editor
Peter Ensenberger — Photography Director     Mary Winkelman Velgos — Art Director     Cindy Mackey — Production Director

Printed in Singapore.   Library of Congress Catalog Number 96-80517   ISBN 0-916179-62-1

# Preface

**W**ith color photography that primes the senses and travelogues that focus on family fun, this book highlights Arizona's Parkways, Historic, and Scenic Roads program begun in 1982.

After extensive research, the Arizona Transportation Board designated various road segments as parkway, historic, or scenic. Designated segments are marked by a special sign (see page 1).

Most of these segments begin and end away from population centers. But touring motorists cannot beam themselves to the start of each designated segment. So, the tours described in this book begin and end in a city or town, and many of them are designed as loops to expose travelers to more scenery than they would see in an out-and-back trip on the same road. In addition, each tour includes descriptions and information about sights to see and things to do along or near the tour route.

This book complements two previous guides from *Arizona Highways:* the best-selling *Travel Arizona II* and *Travel Arizona: The Back Roads.*

We wish to also acknowledge the help and support of the Federal Highway Administration and of Roadside Development Services, Arizona Department of Transportation.

— *Bob Albano*

(PRECEDING PANEL, PAGES 4-5) *Mount Hayden dominates the view from Point Imperial at the North Rim of the Grand Canyon.* RANDY A. PRENTICE
(LEFT) *A brilliant sunset silhouettes Joshua trees along the Joshua Forest Scenic Road.* JACK DYKINGA

# Introduction

**A**rizona enjoys celebrity status as a land with stunning and diverse physical features.

This robust landscape draws archaeologists, filmmakers, hikers, photographers, boaters, and bird-watchers, to name a few. They find adventure in the deserts — the Sonoran, Chihuahuan, and Mohave — mountains and forests; riparian woodlands; and plateaus, canyons, and valleys with rust-colored monoliths. Each year, nearly five million people converge upon the Grand Canyon alone, while another 3.5 million explore the turquoise waters and sandstone shores of Lake Powell. Monument Valley, Sedona, the Coronado Trail, Route 66, the Apache Trail — each conjures up vivid images readily recognizable to most people.

Arizona's history is as rich and colorful as its famous geography. People have lived in this land for 12,000 years. By A.D. 1000, several cultures had formed in the deserts, mountains, and plateaus. In A.D. 1185, about 30 members of the Kayenta Anasazi thrived near the Grand Canyon at Tusayan. The area today probably embraces more visitors than any other archaeological site in the National Park system.

South of Tucson, Spanish explorers pushed north through the Santa Cruz River Valley three centuries ago. Jesuit priest Eusebio Francisco Kino began missionary efforts at Guevavi and Tumacácori in 1691 before moving north to San Xavier del Bac. These mission sites, in various stages of preservation, remain today for us to study in appreciable amazement.

Arizona was designated a territory of the United States in 1863. For much of the remainder of the century the territory was gripped by battles to civilize the land — battles between the Army and Indians, and the law-abiding and the renegades.

Arizona's landscape and battles have been the basis of many movies. Cowboy star Tom Mix was living in Prescott and filming there in 1913. In the 1930s, according to some accounts, Clark Gable and Carole Lombard stayed briefly at the Oatman Hotel after they were married in Kingman. Later, Hollywood returned to Oatman to film major segments of *How the West Was Won.* Many of the false building fronts from the movie set are still standing, as is the now-famous honeymoon hotel. Before that filming, the distinctive sandstone monoliths of Monument Valley served as the backdrop in 1939 for John Ford's epic Western, *Stagecoach,* which cast a young John Wayne as Ringo Kid. In the 1950s, the San Rafael Valley near Sonoita was convincingly cast as Oklahoma, and the Rodgers & Hammerstein musical classic came to the silver screen.

For eight months my family and I spent weekends traveling each of the routes in this book. Besides me, there was Michael, 9, and Kelsey (who was 4, but thought she was considerably older). Now and then, Chuck and I even managed trips alone. We browsed at trading posts, read the roadside markers, and admired the mountainsides, plant and animal life, and sunrises and sunsets. In the process, we developed a keen appreciation for Arizona and met some interesting, genuinely nice people.

While Kelsey remembers everything as "pretty," the rest of us learned that there was a lot more to what we had seen than pleasing appearances. Every town, canyon, and river offered the chance to step back in time. We discovered an Arizona as rich in history and culture as it is in beauty.

Each roadway herein offers the opportunity for all travelers to experience the same time warp. Designated as parkways, historic, and scenic roads, they are preserved and protected for their notably visual and cultural qualities. Each presents some of the most striking landscape you're likely ever to find.

But more so, these roads invite travelers to share the history of Arizona, to celebrate the past, and to revel in the days when Arizona was still the "Old West."

— *Paula Searcy*

(OPPOSITE PAGE) *Shadows cast by clouds under a setting sun help define the shapes and tones of East and West Mitten buttes in Monument Valley.* TOM DANIELSEN

# Patagonia-Sonoita Scenic Road

*WHERE THE PADRES ONCE WALKED*

Photographs by Randy A. Prentice

**Name:** Patagonia-Sonoita Scenic Road.

**Route:** State Routes 82 and 83.

**Mileage:** Tucson to Nogales, 63 miles; Nogales to Patagonia, Sonoita, I-10 at Exit 281, and Tucson, 68 miles.

**Time to allow:** Four to five hours.

**Elevation:** About 2,400 feet at Tucson to about 4,900 feet at Sonoita.

**Overview:** This loop drive takes you by historic sites, including a missile museum and old missions, and into the Santa Cruz River basin in an area marked by broad, rolling valleys, mesquite-grassland vegetation, narrow canyons, and mountain ranges.

On an early Saturday morning in August, we arose earlier and more excited than usual. We were about to embark on our first journey since I had been assigned to write this book, and we were eager to begin our trip.

What would we find? From research I had done, it seemed there was an awful lot in the state that we had never encountered even though we had lived in Arizona for years. Excitement surged through us at the prospect of driving an especially scenic road and visiting historic, cultural, and recreational sites.

The Patagonia-Sonoita Scenic Road stretches from just northeast of Nogales to Interstate 10. I decided to make my trip a loop drive by driving from Tucson to Nogales, then to Patagonia, Sonoita, I-10, and back to Tucson. So, after breakfast we headed south from Tucson on Interstate 19 toward Nogales.

We stopped off at Mission San Xavier del Bac, about 10 miles south of downtown Tucson, and I told Michael and Kelsey, ages 9 and almost 4, how Native Americans had traveled nearly the same route we would be following as they traded along the Rio Santa Cruz. And how, in 1691, Padre Eusebio Francisco Kino, a priest, entered Arizona using the same path to establish missions at Guevavi, Tumacácori, and, later, San Xavier del Bac, which still serves an Indian congregation.

We were impressed by the Spanish mission architecture. A huge dome rests gracefully atop one tower, while the other tower remains unfinished to this day. Large fields spread out beyond the mission's walls where residents of

(OPPOSITE PAGE) *Dusk puts a blanket of serenity on Mission San Xavier del Bac, often called the White Dove of the Desert.*
(ABOVE, RIGHT) *Mesquite trees dot the rolling hills near Salero Mine Road north of Patagonia.*
(ABOVE) *A continuous game of "cat and mouse" plays out on the ornate facade above the front door of San Xavier Mission. Legend says the world will end when the cat catches the mouse.*

the San Xavier Indian Reservation grow crops. A cat and mouse are frozen in a continuous game of chase on each of two concrete columns above the ornate door. It's said that when the cat catches the mouse, the world will end. As I walked away from the mission, I silently prayed, "Godspeed to the mouse."

Continuing south on I-19, we stopped at the Titan II Missile Museum, one of 18 missile sites the U.S. Air Force maintained near Tucson from 1963 until 1982, and the only one remaining today in the United States. All other sites were destroyed by the late 1980s. The museum offers visitors the chance to see a 103-foot Titan missile as it would have appeared 30 years ago when it stood on alert during the Cold War — minus the plutonium warhead, of course.

A tour of the site lasts about one hour and takes you 35 feet underground to the missile control center. Michael sat in the control seat as the launch code was entered; then he turned one key while a guide turned another, "launching" the missile into action. We were all chilled as alarms resounded throughout the silo and across the desert. I felt an uneasy thrill, and thought again of the cat and mouse playing their game, just up the road.

Heading south again on I-19, we passed the startlingly beautiful Santa Rita Mountains to the east, with Mount Wrightson crowning the range at 9,453 feet. Madera Canyon (go east at Exit 63), within the range, offers excellent hiking, camping, sight-seeing and bird-watching. Among the approximately 200 species of birds that spend

at least a part of the year in the canyon are the colorful elegant trogon, broad-billed hummingbird, and the sulphur-bellied flycatcher.

The hills on the west side of the highway make up the Sierrita Mountains. Farther south, we passed the Tumacácori Mountains, again to the west, followed by the Atascosa Mountains as we neared Rio Rico.

At Exit 34, a frontage road on the east side of the highway leads to Tubac and Tumacácori. Steeped in Hispanic culture and Arizona history, the area includes a mission, Tubac Presidio State Historic Park, an old cemetery, a part of a trail forged in the 1770s by Spanish explorer Juan Bautista de Anza, and more than 80 shops and studios featuring arts and crafts. Tubac's history dates to 1752 when it housed Spanish soldiers protecting settlers from Apache Indians. Remnants of that fort are preserved in the park.

South of Tubac and Tumacácori the scenic road begins at State Route 82 in Nogales and heads northeast.

(ABOVE) *Mount Wrightson, at 9,453 feet the tallest peak in southern Arizona, reigns over an expanse of Sonoran Desert laced with ocotillo, prickly pear, and native grass.*
(OPPOSITE PAGE, TOP) *Wooden gargoyles guard the wine-tasting bar at Arizona Vineyards Winery northeast of Nogales.*
(OPPOSITE PAGE, BOTTOM) *Grosvenor Hills cast shadows on Patagonia Lake as three residents of Patagonia Lake State Park waddle along.*

On the edge of town we stopped at the Arizona Vineyards Winery. Inside are wooden gargoyles and other 16th-century artifacts rescued from a Catholic church in Bali, along with an assortment of other interesting items. The wine is made right there in huge wood and cement vats, and there's a colorfully decorated little bar set up in the back for tasting the home-grown products.

While there, we met Bob Segelbaum and his friend, who was visiting from New York. As we sat around sipping a variety of wines, I told them about the book and asked the New Yorker how he liked Arizona. "I come here to get away from the heat, if you can believe that," he replied. I didn't know what to think about that. Not many people travel to southern Arizona in August to escape the heat, but then I don't know anything about the climate in New York either. Our new friend said it's pretty miserable there.

After purchasing three bottles of wine, we said good-bye and continued on our way. The imposing Patagonia Mountains rose on the right, shrouding several old mining camps, now ghost towns. Among them are Washington Camp, Duquesne, and Harshaw. You can drive back to them on dirt roads if the weather has been good — check road conditions first.

For the next 50 or so miles I was amazed that the countryside held so much beauty. But there it was. Right after leaving Nogales, the highway swept through artistically rugged rock outcroppings, and rolled along the edges of several small canyons filled with lush, green vegetation. Perfect, peaceful biking territory, I assumed, because I counted about six or seven cyclists before the terrain flattened out.

Next came rolling grasslands, with beautiful open fields — cattle-grazing territory. Hollywood movie makers thought this area epitomized Oklahoma as it was in the early 1900s and shot the musical *Oklahoma!* in the San Rafael Valley, located east of the highway.

We dropped in at Patagonia Lake State Park, located about 16 miles north of Nogales and four miles west of the highway. There's a fee for using the park but the ranger let us look around for a dollar. Most of the state parks will let you drive through and look around if you don't plan to get out of your vehicle. This gem features spectacular views of the Santa Rita and Patagonia Mountains and the deep, blue waters of the 265-acre lake on Sonoita Creek. The park offers good camping, hiking trails, fishing (bass, crappie, catfish and bluegills), picnicking, water-skiing, and swimming, and we made a mental note to go back when we had a day to spend at the park.

Returning to State Route 82, we continued northward onto a high (about 4,050 feet) prairie and the quiet, pleasant town of Patagonia. We wished we had made reservations at the Stage Stop Inn so we could stay longer to explore the quaint, old buildings and shops in this town that dates to 1896. Information for visitors is available at Mariposa Books on McKeown Avenue next to the Stage Stop Inn.

Just outside of Patagonia lies a popular spot to view birds and other wildlife — the 320-acre Patagonia-Sonoita Creek Preserve. You know you're there when you see the huge cottonwood stands. Even in town, the hummingbirds flitted everywhere.

Just north of Patagonia, we pulled over at a historical marker announcing that Camp Crittenden once stood nearby. The sign says the camp was established August 10, 1867, as a base for soldiers to protect settlements in the Babocomari, Sonoita, and Santa Cruz valleys against Indian attacks and that Lt. H.B. Cushing was killed in 1871 during a skirmish with Cochise's band of Apaches.

Sonoita was next, with its large rodeo arena and huge grandstand where Chuck's cousin competes frequently. There's a steak house located conveniently at the intersection of State routes 82 and 83 for all the hungry cowpokes — and weary travelers, too. There are other fine eateries, catering to many different tastes.

The countryside around Sonoita is so peaceful, grassy, and green. I looked back across the highway at the Santa Ritas, visible again now that we had come around in a loop, and the storm clouds were still brewing over the peaks. The Sonoita Valley stretched out before us, with its tall grasses waving in the breeze. The kids hopped around excitedly, partly impressed with what they saw and partly glad just to be out of the car.

Leaving Sonoita, we traveled northward on 83, the second half of the Patagonia-Sonoita Scenic Road. Once again, the grasslands rolled gently away from the road, stretching endlessly toward the mountains on the horizon. In this area the movie *Giant* was filmed.

About seven miles north of Sonoita, we passed through land that once was a part of the sprawling Empire Ranch, admiring the Empire Mountains in the distance north of us. Now it's named the Empire-Cienega Resource Conservation Area and is administered by the federal Bureau of Land Management. If you drive into the area, you'll see wildflowers, grasslands, oak woodlands, and marshy areas — they are called cienegas — lined with huge cottonwoods. The area also is a preserve for animals such as deer, antelope, javelina, and more than 150 species of birds.

There's a sign on the right (east) side of the highway

(BELOW) *Agave (century) plants grow for a dozen or more years before sprouting flower stalks.*
(OPPOSITE PAGE) *Touring Colossal Cave is an option for travelers after the Patagonia-Sonoita Scenic Road trip.*

marking a road leading into the area. The road meanders for 10 or so miles, passing the old ranch headquarters.

Farther north on 83, ocotillos grew in thick abundance across the fields, and the mountains seemed to reach up into the clouds. We were disappointed to see the sign announcing I-10 show up so quickly at the roadside that leads into the heart of the area.

Depending on how much time you allot for this trip, the fun doesn't have to end here. Colossal Cave is nearby, on I-10 (just follow the signs), offering tours back into a wonderful, dry limestone cave where the temperature is always about 70 degrees, and, according to legend, $60,000 in gold is hidden somewhere within! We went there with the kids, and everyone had a good time. Hang onto the little ones — there are some pretty deep caverns where you could lose a tiny tyke.

From Colossal Cave, you can return to Tucson either on I-10 or via Colossal Cave Road and Old Spanish Trail, a drive that takes you through Saguaro National Park East. Signs will direct you, so you can pick the route you want.

Those who want to head to Benson, about 30 minutes southeast of Exit 281, might ride the San Pedro & Southwestern Railroad train from Benson to Charleston. It's a 27-mile four-hour trip, with fantastic views of the Dragoon Mountains, San Pedro Valley, the Whetstone Mountains, and the San Pedro National Riparian Conservation Area.

# When You Go

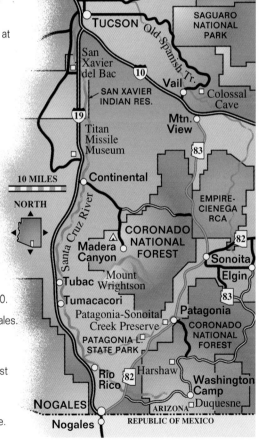

**Southeastern Arizona wineries:** Check with the Patagonia Community Association: recording, 520-394-0060; www.theriver.com/Public/patagoniaaz/

**Colossal Cave:** Take Interstate 10 east 22 miles from downtown Tucson and turn north at Exit 279. Fee. Tours start every half hour and last 45 to 50 minutes. 520-791-7677.

**Coronado National Forest Headquarters, Tucson:** Call about maps, hiking, camping, etc. in the forest, which has segments throughout southern Arizona. 520-670-4552.

**Empire-Cienega Resource Conservation Area:** Open year-round but has no water or facilities. Hike, picnic, or camp. Great bird-watching. 520-722-4289.

**Madera Canyon:** From I-19 take Exit 63 and drive west about 13 miles. Santa Rita Lodge: 520-625-8746.

**Mission San Xavier del Bac:** Open daily, 8 a.m. to 5 p.m. Donations accepted. Take I-19 south from Tucson, turn off on Exit 92, and follow the signs. 520-294-2624.

**Nogales-Santa Cruz County Chamber of Commerce:** 520-287-3685.

**Patagonia Lake State Park:** Camping, RV hookups, hiking, swimming, fishing. Call ahead on summer weekends, as park fills up. About 10 miles northeast of Nogales, turn west onto Patagonia Lake Road. 520-287-6965.

**Patagonia-Sonoita Creek Preserve:** No pets or camping. In Patagonia, turn west on Fourth Avenue, go two blocks, turn left, go 1.5 miles. Call for days, times. 520-394-2400.

**Pimería Alta Historical Society Museum:** Grand Avenue and Crawford Street, Nogales. Artifacts show the history on both sides of the border in what the Spanish called Pimería Alta — home of the upper Pima Indians. Call for days and times. 520-287-4621.

**Titan II Missile Museum:** Call for days and times. One-hour tours begin at 9 a.m. Last tour departs at 4 p.m. Fee. From Tucson take I-19 south to Exit 69. 520-625-7736.

**Regional annual events:** Patagonia Heritage Festival, Memorial Day weekend, May. Sonoita Quarter Horse Show, nation's oldest quarter horse show, first weekend in June. Patagonia Fall Festival, October. Fiesta de Tumacacori, first weekend in December, Tumacacori National Historical Park.

**Tumacacori National Historical Park:** Take I-19 about 45 miles south from Tucson, turn off on Exit 29, and follow the signs. 520-398-2341. www.nps.gov/tuma/

**Tubac Presidio State Historic Park:** Take I-19 about 45 miles south from Tucson at Exit 34. 520-398-2252. www.pr.state.az.us

# Sky Island Scenic Byway

**Photographs by Randy A. Prentice**

**Name:** Sky Island Scenic Byway.

**Route:** Hitchcock Highway, also called Mount Lemmon Road and Catalina Highway.

**Mileage:** Tucson to Summmerhaven, 25 miles.

**Time to allow:** Three to four hours.

**Elevation:** 2,400 feet to nearly 9,200 feet. You'll encounter snow in the winter but the paved road is kept plowed.

**Overview:** This "sky island" drive takes you from the floor of the Sonoran Desert to the village of Summerhaven and Mount Lemmon, which has hiking trails, camping and picnic sites, and a ski area. The byway is not a part of the state's scenic road system, but it carries the scenic designation of the U.S. Forest Service. This paved, two-lane road consists of one curve or switchback after another.

October reigns as one of the most beautiful times in Arizona. Temperatures in the deserts gradually, mercifully, become cooler, while trees in the mountain regions dress themselves in bright red, yellow, and orange hues. And one lovely, late morning, under a warm, desert sun, Chuck, Michael, Kelsey, and I left downtown Tucson and drove toward the Santa Catalina Mountains, northeast of town.

We were bound for the Catalina Highway — officially named the Hitchcock Highway after a former postmaster general and Tucson newspaper editor who campaigned for construction of the road. Often locally called the Mount Lemmon Road, this pathway is designated by the U.S. Forest Service and Pima County as Sky Island Scenic Byway. I was particularly excited about this drive — I had admired the Santa Catalina Mountains many times during trips to Tucson, but had never driven into them.

The mountain range borders the north edge of Tucson, providing a scenic backdrop for the sprawling desert city. Locals and visitors alike refer to these mountains as an island in the desert, offering a cool escape from the blistering summer sun and a southwestern location to enjoy winter snows.

Originally built by prison laborers in the 1930s and '40s, the Catalina Highway winds lazily up the southern face of the Santa Catalinas, located within the Coronado National Forest. Originating among the giant saguaros of the Sonoran Desert, at an elevation of about 2,400 feet, the route climbs more than 6,000 feet into grasslands, oak woodlands, and ponderosa pine forests, then tops out at just over 9,000 feet in a mixed conifer woodland. Outdoors enthusiasts liken the drive to a trip from Mexico to Canada — in just a few hours.

Beautiful views of Tanque Verde Valley (looking south from the road), the San Pedro River Valley (looking east), and Molino Canyon lend themselves easily to travelers climbing the winding route along heavily

(OPPOSITE PAGE) *Windy Point offers one of the more dramatic vistas along the Sky Island Scenic Byway in the Santa Catalina Mountains north of Tucson. Here, you're looking west at sunset.*
(ABOVE) *Sunflowers and an observatory operated by the University of Arizona share a field in the Bear Wallow area of the Santa Catalina Mountains.*

vegetated mountainsides. Views of Tucson, and of numerous unusual rock formations such as Goosehead Rock, are visible from overlooks at several points along the highway.

In 1881, botanist John Gil Lemmon and his bride, Sarah, ventured into the mountains to look for new plant species. They located over 100 new species, and gave their name to the range's highest peak, Mount Lemmon, which rises to 9,157 feet.

The roots of Summerhaven trace to 1910, when Frank Weber established a 160-acre homestead near Mount Lemmon. But access to the mountaintop remained limited to a rugged trail. Residents had to be supplied by pack trains.

The Great Depression and World War II slowed recreation and building in the mountains for a while, but editor Frank Harris Hitchcock revived interest in the project and convinced officials to use prison labor to complete a road to the top. The road took nearly 20 years to complete, reaching Soldier Camp in 1946. Finally, in 1951, the road was surfaced.

Recreation facilities were upgraded as the road was completed. New scenic turnouts, picnic areas, and campgrounds sprang up or received face-lifts at Molino Basin, Bear Canyon, Rose Canyon, Inspiration Rock, Soldier Camp, and Marshall Gulch. In the summer of

1948, approximately 2,000 people drove up the highway on weekends. Ten years later, that number skyrocketed to over 380,000 people a year.

The Mount Lemmon drive requires visitors to come prepared for warm, cool, and possibly cold temperatures. When we left Tucson, all of us had on short sleeves. When we stopped to walk around at the Palisades Visitors Center, we put on sweatshirts. And when we stepped from the car at the ski area near the summit, we hurriedly donned jackets. Suddenly, it seemed it was freezing.

There was no snow yet, so ski season hadn't arrived, but we took a scenic ski lift ride up and down the mountain, something I highly recommend, especially to first-time visitors. Kelsey and I cuddled together in one chair, while Michael and Chuck tried to appear manly, and not cold at all, as they sat side by side in another chair. What a thrill to dangle above the treetops that way!

The mountain was ablaze in glorious red and gold, and when we exhaled, puffy clouds formed right in front of our faces. Wood smoke from nearby cabins drifted in the air.

After the chairlift ride, we drove into Summerhaven. It's a small town filled with cabins, some small stores, and a school. The town depends heavily on tourism, but the year-round population is quite evident, too.

On the way down the mountain, we stopped at Rose Canyon, which has a campground and seven-acre lake set in a pine forest. Here, less than 20 miles from the desert, people can fish the cold waters for trout and enjoy hiking and other outdoor activities.

The drive takes about an hour each way without stopping, so allow a day to wander through the campgrounds, enjoy the hiking trails, pick berries, and admire the scenic views. Facilities are limited once you begin the drive, so gas up in Tucson and take at least a gallon of water and some food if you want to snack on the way up. Better yet, enjoy a picnic lunch on the cool mountain slopes. ✍

(OPPOSITE PAGE) *The Bear Wallow area of the Santa Catalina Mountains presents a pleasant setting for an autumn stroll under a canopy of reds and yellows.*
(ABOVE) *Ponderosa pine trees tower over a boy fishing at Rose Canyon Lake, located just off the Mount Lemmon Highway at an elevation of about 7,000 feet.*

## When You Go

**Coronado National Forest, Santa Catalina Ranger Station:** Sabino Canyon, 520-749-8700.

**Mount Lemmon Ski Valley:** Skyride open year-round. Downhill skiing and snowboarding in winter. Restaurant, snack bar, gift shop, and equipment rental. 520-576-1400.

**Mount Lemmon lodging and food:**

Alpine Lodge: 520-576-1544.

Aspen Trail bed and breakfast: 520-576-1558.

Mount Lemmon Suites & Fine Crafts: 520-576-1664.

Summerhaven Coffee House: 520-576-1586

**Metro Tucson Convention and Visitors Bureau:** 130 S. Scott Ave., Tucson 85701. Call 520-624-1817 or 800-638-8350.

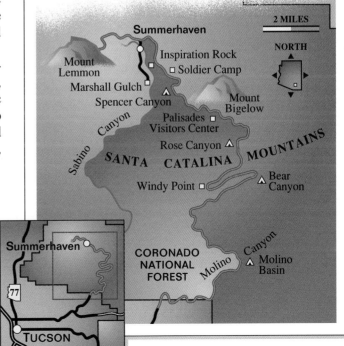

# Apache Trail Historic Road

**Photographs by Jerry Sieve**

The Apache Trail, located east of Metropolitan Phoenix, possibly can boast of having the most historical, cultural, and scenic significance ever packed into 41 miles of roadway, 25 of which are graded gravel and dirt. The route follows the Salt River, believed to have been the backbone of Salado and Hohokam civilizations existing in the area between A.D. 900 and A.D. 1400. Many people also believe that Phoenix and central Arizona never would have developed to the extent they have without harnessing the power and water of this river through the construction of Roosevelt Dam.

The Apache Trail, most of which is in the Tonto National Forest, ends near Roosevelt Lake, about 30 miles from where the Gila-Pinal Scenic Drive begins just outside of Globe, so we decided to make a loop drive and spare ourselves the return trip over Fish Creek Hill. (More about the hill later.) Chuck, Kelsey, and I left on a Thursday and planned to return the following Monday so we would have plenty of time. We promised Michael pictures and a souvenir, since he had to remain behind due to a demanding hockey schedule.

The trail begins east of Phoenix in Apache Junction. Take U.S. Route 60 (the Superstition Freeway) to State Route 88 (Idaho Road) and go north to the start of the scenic road.

After a few minutes on the trail, we stopped at Goldfield Ghost Town, constructed to show tourists what a Western mining town might have looked like. The actual town of Goldfield once stood very near to today's site. In the 1880s numerous local gold mines with names like Mammoth, Tom Thumb, Mother Hubbard, and Black King began yielding millions of dollars in gold ore, and in 1893 the town site was laid out. Two years later, torrential rain flooded the mine shafts. Owners tried to pump the water out but gave up when they realized it would only go down about an inch a year. Indians had long claimed that mining operations on the sacred mountains angered their Thunder God. They saw the flooding as his way of removing the white men from the land. By 1899 Goldfield was a ghost town.

In the current version of Goldfield, visitors can

**Name:** Apache Trail Historic Road.

**Route:** State Route 88.

**Mileage:** Apache Junction to Tortilla Flat and Roosevelt Dam and Lake, 42 miles. Roosevelt to Globe-Miami, 30 miles.

**Time to allow:** Two to three hours.

**Elevation:** About 1,700 feet at Apache Junction; about 3,050 feet atop Fish Creek Hill; about 2,400 feet at Roosevelt Lake.

**Overview:** Flanking the Superstition Mountains, fabled site of the elusive Lost Dutchman Mine, this ancient trail follows the Salt River. A few miles into the trip you'll be driving between the Superstition Wilderness (on your right) and Four Peaks Wilderness (on your left). Along the way you can enjoy three lakes with marinas. Much of the trail is graded gravel and dirt, but a passenger vehicle can safely traverse the road. At the end of the drive you are just a few miles from the Gila-Pinal Scenic Road, which returns you to metropolitan Phoenix (see Page 25).

*(OPPOSITE PAGE) Brittlebush and pink asters decorate the desert floor below the Superstition Mountains, which flank a section of the Apache Trail.*
*(ABOVE) Goldfield re-creates an 1800s mining town at the base of the Superstition Mountains.*

wander through old-time buildings, browse the gift shops, eat at a steak house, or have a favorite friend or loved one arrested and then shot or hanged in public in front of the jail. There's also a live rattlesnake exhibit. Chuck and Kelsey enjoyed that attraction together, while I waited outside hoping no snaky escapees would come slithering out.

Lost Dutchman State Park is just up the road from Goldfield, nestled around the base of the Superstition Mountains. We asked the gate attendant if we could drive through the park without paying a fee and he waved us through. The park offers camping and hiking trails and plenty of room to wander about, speculating on the location of Jacob Waltz's Lost Dutchman Gold Mine. History buffs think the mine lies in the Superstitions or possibly over in Goldfield across the highway.

There has been plenty of evidence that gold exists in the mountains, even though they are volcanic in origin and are not supposed to be the kind of formation that contains precious metal. Yet geologists acknowledge that if a vent occurred somewhere during an eruption, it would be possible for a vein to form there.

Miguel Peralta, a wealthy Mexican cattle rancher, reportedly found a rich gold mine up in the mountains, and mined it until Mexico signed the Treaty of Guadalupe Hidalgo ceding Arizona to the United States in 1848. He was killed by Indians as he tried to remove a last load of ore.

After Peralta, several other miners probed the mountains for gold. Some were successful, but most of them met with disastrous fates. But they kept trying, including legendary Jacob Waltz, who was called Dutchman. But he was not Dutch. He was German, a Deutchman not a Dutchman. Just before he died in Phoenix in 1891, he said the opening of the mine shaft could be found by watching where the shadow of Weavers Needle rested at four o'clock in the afternoon. Alas, that shadow moves every day of the year. But to this day adventurers still search for the Dutchman's lost mine.

Back on State Route 88, we continued northeast. Less than a half mile from the park entrance, Forest Service Road 78 bears right from State 88. About 2.5 miles down the forest road there are trails leading into the Superstition Wilderness.

We stayed on the paved road and at about Milepost 203 came to a point with an excellent view of Weavers Needle, elevation 4,535 feet.

Just beyond Milepost 208 we saw how Canyon Lake got its name. It has some sandy beaches on the roadside but the far side of the lake is flanked by steep canyon walls. There's a marina with a restaurant here and picnicking and camping facilities.

Driving on, we crossed two single-lane bridges (the turnoff to the marina is just beyond the second bridge) and came to Tortilla Flat. Tortilla Flat draws its name from the flat mountains in which it sits.

The settlement has a general store, a restaurant, and a gift shop. Inside the restaurant and store, visitors have written their names and dates of their visits on dollar bills, then stapled them to the walls. As he took our lunch order, the waiter said there are more than 15,000 bills in the restaurant, and that's been just since 1989, when the place burned down.

A little less than nine miles from Tortilla Flat looms Fish Creek Hill. By now, you have run out of pavement, but passenger cars can readily travel the graded road.

The advice given me before I left on this trip was to drive Apache Trail from west to east. That way, when I traversed Fish Creek Hill, I would be away from the perilous edge cut from a cliff for nearly two twisting miles. There's a sheer drop of hundreds of feet along the outside edge of the road.

Just before you get to the hill there's a place to park

(BELOW) *Roosevelt Dam impounds waters of the Salt River and Tonto Creek. Dedicated in 1911, the masonry dam underwent a renovation completed in 1996. This view shows the outflow side of the dam.*
(OPPOSITE PAGE) A *boater heads up Apache Lake with the Apache Trail visible on the right.*

on the left. A short trail leads to a ridge where you will get an imposing overview of Fish Creek Canyon. There likely will be birds soaring overhead — ravens and hawks.

About halfway through Fish Creek Hill, there is a stable that offers trail rides in the area, and just after that — just beyond Milepost 227, the Forest Service road (FR 212) to Reavis Ranch Trailhead appears on the right, beckoning hikers to give it a go on foot. The trailhead is almost three miles from the junction. You'll need a high clearance vehicle to travel this road.

In less than two miles from this junction you'll get an overview of Apache Lake. For the next 10 or so miles you'll be flanking the lake with the Four Peaks Wilderness in the Mazatzal Mountains sprawling on the other side of it.

The road climbs toward Roosevelt Dam. Completed in 1911 and modified in the 1990s, this masonry structure is nearly 360 feet tall. Driving the last mile or so of the Apache Trail is a thrill as you twist your way up to the top of the dam.

We stayed at Roosevelt Lake Resort, located 12 miles southeast of the dam off State Route 88. Owner Judy Leach and her family have run the place for the past 18 years, and Judy said it's pretty much the same as it was then. Weekends are always busy. Fishermen flock there from October until about March or April. That's when the watersport crowd starts coming, and they keep the place filled until October, when it starts all over.

We joked about the drive, and Judy told me how huge Greyhound tour buses used to bring busloads of passengers over Fish Creek Hill to the resort. She heard more than one passenger exclaim, "That was great! But do we have to go back that way?"

Our room was nice, the food was good, and Kelsey had a good time playing with the ducks hanging around the pond out back. One of the waitresses showed her a turtle sunning itself on a small island, and she thought that was especially neat. ◪

## When You Go

**Apache Lake Marina:** Fee. Facilities include setups for RV and tent camping, motel, restaurant, and store. 520-467-2511.

**Canyon Lake Marina:** Fee. Daytime and dinner cruises around the lake. 602-944-6504.

**Goldfield Ghost Town:** Open daily, 10 a.m. to 5 p.m. 480-983-0333.

**Lost Dutchman State Park:** Fee. Picnicking, camping, and day-hiking at base of Superstitions. 480-982-4485.

**Roosevelt Lake Marina:** Fee. Boat rentals, camping, other services. 520-467-2245.

**Roosevelt Lake Resort:** Motel, trailer park, and restaurant. 520-467-2276.

**Roosevelt Lake Visitors Center:** Located on State Route 88 a little over a mile east (bear right) of 88's junction with State Route 188. Open daily from 7:30 a.m. to 4:30 p.m. 520-467-3200.

**Tonto National Forest, Mesa District:** Maps and information on camping, hiking, and facilities in the forest. 480-610-3300.

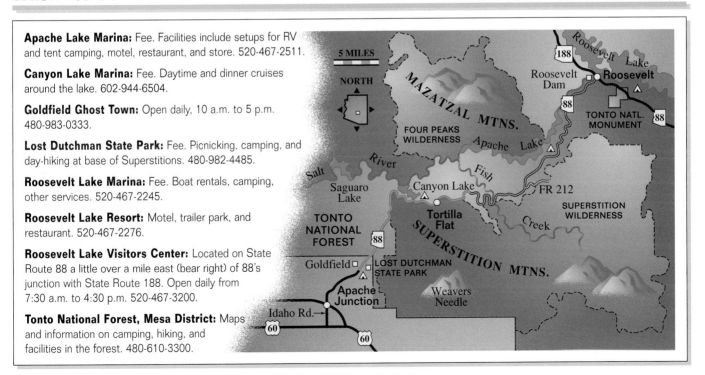

# Gila-Pinal Scenic Road

**Photographs by Jerry Sieve**

**A**fter completing the Apache Trail drive and spending the night by Roosevelt Lake, we backtracked along State Route 88 to Tonto National Monument, just a few miles south of the Apache Trail junction.

The monument protects and interprets a remarkably intact cliff dwelling ruin built by people of the Salado culture about 700 years ago. The half-mile uphill hike takes you to the lower site, and you can walk through the ruin. Allow about an hour for the hike and viewing. Guides will lead you up to the upper ruin. You can get a good view of the site, but you can't walk through it.

The Globe-Miami area is only a half-hour or so drive from the ruins. Take State 88 south to U.S. Route 60 and turn left for Globe, a copper mining center settled in 1876.

The highway takes you right to the historic section of Globe, including a restored courthouse and other buildings dating to the turn of the century and before.

We stopped at Besh-Ba-Gowah Archaeological Park, where visitors enter the ruin through the same central corridor the original Salado Indians used and then walk through the rooms of the ancient structure, climb the ladders into top rooms, examine pottery and utensils, and really get a feel for how the people lived when the site was inhabited in the period A.D. 1225 to 1400. Evidence of earlier Hohokam pit houses remain on the site as well.

We returned to U.S. 60 and the start of the Gila-Pinal Scenic Road, which is at Milepost 240 just west of Miami. This town got its start as a mining camp. Black Jack Newman named his mining camp Mima in honor of his fiancée, Mima Tune. Eventually, due to pressure from a group of miners from Miami, Ohio, the name was corrupted and became Miami.

Bloody Tanks Wash courses through Miami. According to some accounts, the wash was the site in 1864 of a fight between a militia, led by Colonel King Woolsey, and Apaches. Supposedly, the two groups were to meet to exchange gifts and talk. Both sides were armed and the

**Name:** Gila-Pinal Scenic Road.

**Route:** U.S. Route 60.

**Mileage:** Globe-Miami to Superior and Florence Junction, 39 miles.

**Time to allow:** Two to three hours.

**Elevation:** About 3,500 feet at Globe-Miami; about 1,300 feet at Florence Junction. Snow falls occasionally in the mountains.

**Overview:** This year-round drive complements the Apache Trail trek (see Page 21), completing a loop that starts and ends east of Phoenix. The Gila-Pinal celebrates the wonder and diversity of the Arizona landscape. On the east, it starts on the northern flank of the Pinal Mountains, rolls through miles of undulating lands and steep canyons with unusual rock outcroppings, and ends with panoramic views of the Sonoran Desert. Avoid driving this route east to west in the late afternoon, otherwise you'll be staring into the sun most of the way.

(OPPOSITE PAGE) *This hiker heads to Indian ruins in the Tonto National Monument, set amid stately saguaro cactuses next to Roosevelt Lake.*
(ABOVE) *Several cactus varieties thrive in Barkley Basin in the Superstition Wilderness.*
(RIGHT) *In the Tonto National Monument, sunrise illuminates an entry to dwellings (the lower ruins) once occupied by the Salado people.*

militiamen fired first. Reportedly, 19 Indians were shot and their blood stained the water, giving the wash its name.

Elsewhere in Miami, Chuck was impressed by the copper mining waste piled into grayish, terraced mountains.

At this point the road begins climbing to an elevation of about 4,200 feet. Off to our left we saw Pinal Peak, which at 7,812 feet is the highest in the Pinal range.

By Milepost 229 we were in the midst of Devils Canyon, looking down onto a mesquite and paloverde covered floor, then out across the rugged landscape toward cliffs slowly eroding above the valley. Vegetation is dense and green, and riparian areas can be seen along several creeks, Ash, Queen, and Arnett among them.

I thought the views of Picket Post Mountain and Apache Leap were stunning. They are visible to the south off and on for most of the drive but especially beautiful once you near Superior.

Squinting through the bright sun toward Apache Leap in the Dripping Spring Mountains, I recalled that Apache Leap draws its name from an undocumented story about 75 Apache warriors who jumped to their deaths from the butte rather than face capture by soldiers.

Picket Post Mountain was named after a military camp that was near the 4,370-foot lookout point.

Just west of Superior, we stopped at Boyce Thompson Southwestern Arboretum State Park. We strolled through the arboretum, marveling at the unique desert life from all around the world. Founded in 1924 by mining magnate William Boyce Thompson, the arboretum includes a mosaic of gardens, a desert lake, sheer mountain cliffs, panoramic vistas, and miles of easy nature trails.

The end of the scenic drive rounds out at Milepost 214 on the southern side of the Superstition Mountains and affords travelers a spectacular view of the range and Weavers Needle. I couldn't help looking at my watch to see if it was anywhere near four o'clock. ◪

(LEFT) *Weavers Needle juts into the horizon above the Superstition Mountains along the Gila-Pinal Scenic Road. Ocotillo and cholla are among the plants in the foreground.*
(ABOVE) *Dramatic rock formations along the Gila-Pinal Scenic Road characterize Devils Canyon.*
(RIGHT) *The Boyce Thompson Arboretum State Park cultivates many exotic plants from around the world, including the boojum trees and blooming agave pictured here.*

## When You Go

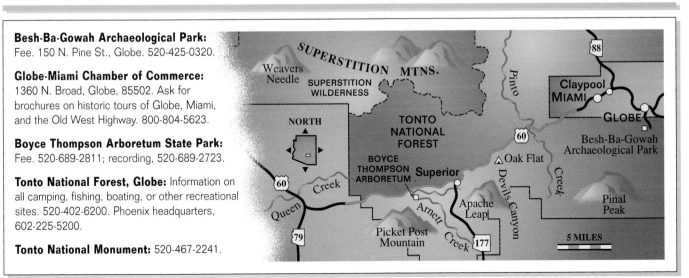

**Besh-Ba-Gowah Archaeological Park:** Fee. 150 N. Pine St., Globe. 520-425-0320.

**Globe-Miami Chamber of Commerce:** 1360 N. Broad, Globe, 85502. Ask for brochures on historic tours of Globe, Miami, and the Old West Highway. 800-804-5623.

**Boyce Thompson Arboretum State Park:** Fee. 520-689-2811; recording, 520-689-2723.

**Tonto National Forest, Globe:** Information on all camping, fishing, boating, or other recreational sites. 520-402-6200. Phoenix headquarters, 602-225-5200.

**Tonto National Monument:** 520-467-2241.

# From Desert to Pines Scenic Byway

State Route 288 begins in the desert south of Theodore Roosevelt Lake, switchbacks up to stands of pine and fir trees in the Sierra Ancha Mountains, and ends on the Mogollon Rim, a densely forested cliff extending east-west across central Arizona for 100 miles. The road sometimes is called the Young Highway because it leads to and through Young, an isolated, unincorporated community at the top of the range.

As the crow flies, the Sierra Ancha Mountains are not far from civilization. The copper mining towns of Globe and Miami are only a couple of hours down the mountain. But relative closeness is meaningless where deep canyons and dense foliage can swallow you. The area is so rough and so sparsely populated that a visitor feels there couldn't possibly be a city within a two-day drive. For some, that feeling is a good one; for others, the opposite holds true, which is a way of saying a drive up the Young Highway is not for everyone.

Most of the road is unpaved. In places the dirt is corrugated like an old-fashioned washboard, and it can be slippery. There are more twists and turns than you'll find in a Stephen King novel, and above 6,000 feet you may hit snow in the winter months. No guardrails separate you from the edge of some very steep canyons.

In short, the Young Highway is potentially a white-knuckle experience. However, driving the road lets you experience unspoiled forests, extravagant foliage in the fall, and the pristine streams and cliffs of the Tonto National Forest.

Dominated by the diminutive, spiny growth of the desert in its lower elevations, the barren face of the range becomes a rich and barely penetrable forest of pines, aspens, Douglas fir, and black walnut trees at its upper reaches. At the base of the mountain, winters are mild and accommodating; at the top of the range, ice and snow are so thick that most side roads are impassable.

To begin this trip, drive 112 miles north of Tucson or 85 miles east of Phoenix to the central Arizona copper mining town of Miami. At the junction of U.S. Route 60

**Name:** From Desert to Tall Pines Scenic Byway.

**Route:** State Route 288 and Forest Route 512 to State Route 260.

**Mileage:** 80 miles.

**Time to allow:** Three to four hours from Globe to State Route 260.

**Elevation:** 2,100 feet at Salt River to 7,600 feet on the Mogollon Rim.

**Overview:** Winds on dirt roads over desert near Roosevelt Lake to pine forests in the Sierra Anchas. Historic Pleasant Valley and Young are located near tour's end.

*(OPPOSITE PAGE) Parker Creek trickles in a canyon below red rock cliffs in the Sierra Ancha Mountains. Fog hazes over Roosevelt Lake in the background.* RANDY A. PRENTICE
*(ABOVE) Viewed from the Sierra Ancha Mountains, the distinctive Four Peaks stand out.*
NICK BEREZENKO

and State Route 88, head north on 88 toward Theodore Roosevelt Lake. State Route 288, the road to Young, begins as a paved highway 15 miles north of the junction in Miami. The road remains paved for the next 11 miles, meandering through a desert that is bright with blossoming paloverde trees and saguaro cactus in late spring. Cross the Salt River near Klondyke Butte, 5.6 miles beyond the start of 288, and begin climbing the narrow winding road until the pavement ends.

The unpaved portion of the road, which begins in the vicinity of Willow Springs, can be handled with an ordinary car, though in places it's rough going.

At Parker Creek, 26.5 miles from the beginning of 288, the vegetation changes abruptly to a thick forest of gray-flecked sycamore trees and huge oaks in a carpet of graceful ferns. The remainder of the route offers spectacular views of rocky pinnacles, ponderosa pines, and other conifers, but the hairpin curves along the road pose danger if you gawk at the scenery. Stop at the many pull-outs to enjoy the fragrant surroundings.

A couple of miles beyond Parker Creek, you can camp or picnic in the pines at 5,400 feet at Rose Creek Campground or the Workman Creek Recreation Area. Workman Creek was named after Herbert Wertman, who lived in the area during the 1880s. As often happened in early Arizona, names came out spelled more or less the way they sounded and Wertman became Workman.

In the 1920s and '30s, a lodge and cabins at Workman Creek were known as the Mesa Settlement because families from Mesa occupied them during the summers to escape temperatures in the Salt River Valley soaring above 100 degrees.

As I approached the Workman Creek cutoff from 288, I looked for signs of the lodge or the cabins but saw nothing. Most of the artifacts of that march toward civilizing (or at least populating) this wild and scenic range had been erased.

Now the forest belongs once more to the black bears, the cautious deer, and adventurous humans — with perhaps one exception: After I turned east from 288 and headed toward the falls, I came upon a YMCA summer camp that has been used for generations by Globe-Miami residents. Beyond that, I drove along, sometimes at a walking pace, on a rocky road that climbed gradually. I'd been told it was possible to drive to the waterfall in Workman Creek, that the road would eventually pass above the falls and go all the way to Aztec Peak, at 7,733 feet the highest point in the range. That information was correct, but the road to the 180-foot waterfall is treacherous in places and should not be driven without a four-wheel drive vehicle. The drive takes 20 to 30 minutes; you can hike the road in about an hour.

When I got to the precipitous cliff at the top of the falls, there were no guard rails, and as I munched an apple I thought how easy it would be for a person with vertigo to topple over the edge. I looked down and saw the tops of leafless aspens and cold, gray sycamores far below me. Only when I returned to town did I hear that a Mesa woman had lost her footing at that very spot a few of years earlier and fallen to her death.

However, time in the Workman Creek-Reynolds Creek area need not always be a harrowing experience. Many miners have worked these precipitous canyons near the falls for years without incident. In 1950 uranium was discovered in the Sierra Anchas and some 14 mines, many of them in the Workman Creek area, were developed. Between 1953 and 1960, those mines produced a total of 2,185 pounds of ore.

There are numerous dirt roads like the one to Workman Creek that take off from 288, but visitors should exercise caution as many are steep and not entirely predictable. One of these roads, Forest Route 609, intersects 288 at a point 9.5 miles north of Workman Creek and leads to Malicious Gap, a low spot between Bear Head and Copper mountains. The name intrigued me, so I asked around and was referred to Frances Conway, who with her husband owns a ranch near the gap. Mrs. Conway said the name was a mistake.

"My husband's out rounding up cattle or he'd tell you himself," she said, "but what he always told me was that some old fellow came through there and stopped for a drink of water, and he said, 'Oh, this is delicious water!' "

How delicious became malicious is something you can think about during the 12.5 miles that separate Malicious Gap turnoff from the Antlers Cafe in beautiful downtown Young, a place where you'll encounter a paved road again. Don't get too excited, though: The pavement only lasts for seven miles and then you'll be back on dirt for 23 miles before the pavement resumes at State Route 260 on the Mogollon Rim. Payson, the nearest large town, is 33 miles to the west on 260.

(LEFT) *Pine needles and sycamore leaves decorate the rocky banks of Workman Creek in the Sierra Ancha Mountains on the scenic road to Young.*
(OPPOSITE PAGE, LEFT) *Last light shrouds the hills above Pleasant Valley and the town of Young. The Mogollon Rim can be seen in the distance.*
BOTH BY RANDY A. PRENTICE
(OPPOSITE PAGE, RIGHT) *The Young Cemetery records some of the history of the Pleasant Valley War, which was a feud involving two families and their supporters.*
NICK BEREZENKO

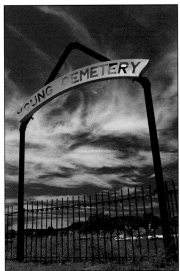

Young looks as peaceful as the Garden of Eden, but from 1887 to 1892 it was a dangerous place because of a bizarre feud that came to be known as the Pleasant Valley War. Zane Grey wrote a fictionalized account of the feud between the Graham and Tewksbury families in a book titled *To The Last Man*. Former *Arizona Highways* editor Don Dedera wrote a nonfiction account of the feud in *A Little War of Our Own*, published in 1987.

In the course of the feud, some 30 people — members of both families and their respective supporters — were killed, and not a single person was convicted of any crime. Never before had the theft of cows produced such vicious and prolonged bloodshed.

Because of the valley's isolated location and its vast hidden canyons and caves, the few lawmen sent over from the county seat at Prescott accomplished little in quelling the violence below the Mogollon Rim. Five years after the feud was presumed to be over, Ed Tewksbury ambushed and killed Tom Graham near Tempe. After a lengthy trial, he was released on a technicality, and became one of the few participants in the saga to die peacefully at home.

Today it would be difficult to find a more crime-free spot on earth than Young, the population of which varies from 300 to 800, depending on the season. You can visit the cemetery and see the graves of some of the victims of the Pleasant Valley War, you can visit an apple orchard you'll see on the right side of the road, or you can stop at the ranger station for the Tonto National Forest, though the ranger is often out in the field.

Once you leave Young, the hard part of the drive is behind you. The remainder of the road up to the rim is wide and smooth and meanders through forests of ponderosa pines. When the pavement ends, you'll be on Forest Route 512, which takes you to the State Route 260. If you're not camping, you can turn west and spend the night in Payson, 33 miles away. ◪

## When You Go

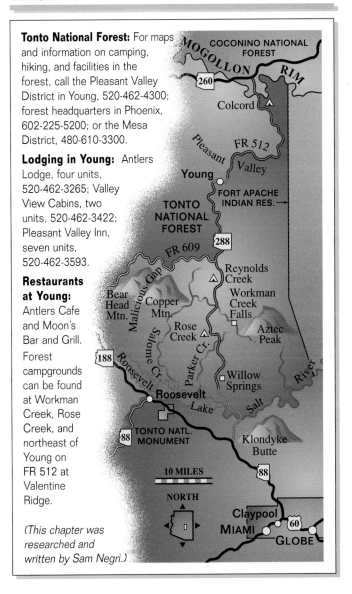

**Tonto National Forest:** For maps and information on camping, hiking, and facilities in the forest, call the Pleasant Valley District in Young, 520-462-4300; forest headquarters in Phoenix, 602-225-5200; or the Mesa District, 480-610-3300.

**Lodging in Young:** Antlers Lodge, four units, 520-462-3265; Valley View Cabins, two units, 520-462-3422; Pleasant Valley Inn, seven units, 520-462-3593.

**Restaurants at Young:** Antlers Cafe and Moon's Bar and Grill. Forest campgrounds can be found at Workman Creek, Rose Creek, and northeast of Young on FR 512 at Valentine Ridge.

*(This chapter was researched and written by Sam Negri.)*

# White River Scenic Road

**Photographs by Jerry Jacka**

Two designated scenic drives in the White Mountains begin at the eastern edge of the Mogollon Rim near the community of Hon-Dah, at the junction of two paved state highways, 260 and 73. One drive, detailed in the following chapter, flows eastward through the White Mountains, the northeast corner of the Fort Apache Indian Reservation, and the Greer Recreation Area. The other, State Route 73, winds down a canyon cradling the North Fork of the White River, and rolls through a grassy, flowery meadow known as Alchesay Flat. This drive through the heart of the Fort Apache Indian Reservation (sometimes called the White Mountain Reservation) gives visitors a glimpse into both the past and present lives of the five groups, called bands, that make the reservation their home.

Chuck and I chose Pinetop as our hub while exploring the two drives. We rented a cozy little cabin at one of the many resorts in the area and on the first morning sat at a tiny table for two, drinking coffee and eating scrambled eggs as we planned the day's events. Then, we were off on State Route 260 heading for the junction of State Route 73, only a few miles southeast of Pinetop. The Hon-Dah casino is at the junction, where we turned right, heading south toward Whiteriver.

**Name:** White River Scenic Road.

**Route:** A loop consisting of State Route 73 and U.S. Route 60.

**Mileage:** 95 miles from Pinetop to Hon-Dah, Whiteriver, Fort Apache, Carrizo, and back to Pinetop.

**Time to allow:** Three to four hours.

**Elevation:** 7,200 feet at Pinetop; 5,300 feet at the town of Whiteriver.

**Overview:** Dropping from the Mogollon Rim, the officially designated scenic route covers about 11 miles and is an excellent choice for a drive to view fall colors. Extending the drive takes travelers to historic Fort Apache, ruins of an ancient village, and back to the top of the Mogollon Rim.

State 73 is one of the few paved roads on the Fort Apache Reservation, locally known as the White Mountain Reservation and home to about 9,000 people. Graded gravel roads as well as unimproved dirt trails form a web through most of the reservation's 1.6 million acres. For the most part, development has spared this land, leaving it filled with dense forests, mountain meadows growing a collage of plants and flowers, wooded canyons, 26 lakes, 800 miles of perennial streams, and acres and acres of wetlands (called cienegas) with bulging cottonwoods and delicate willows. Indeed, this is a feast for those seeking outdoor recreation or scenic-viewing pleasure.

About seven miles south of Hon-Dah, I spotted a wooden cattle chute, weathered gray by time and the elements, about 300 yards off the road on our right. It seemed as though an artist's hand sought to arrange a most pleasing display. The relic rested in a large meadow edged by golden aspens and blazing-red foliage. Closing my eyes, I imagined ranchers astride spunky mounts, driving red-backed, bawling cattle through the old chute.

As we traveled a little farther south, forests of pines stirred my imagination into believing there were tree tops sprouting from nowhere. That's how it seemed from the road because I could not see the lower parts of the trees down in a canyon. I stared in amusement at the tree tops — sort of a bird's-eye view without flying.

(OPPOSITE PAGE) *Small (11 acres) but deep (30 feet), Cooley Lake provides fishing, picnicking, and camping on the Fort Apache Indian Reservation.*
(ABOVE, RIGHT) *Wildflowers now grace Cooley Ranch, once run by an Army scout.*
(ABOVE) *Pines dominate the scene near Hon Dah.*

Cooley Mountain, the dominant peak to our left, was named after Corydon E. Cooley, a scout for General George Crook during the Apache war campaigns. Ironically, this legendary Indian fighter was married to two Apache women at the same time.

Within five miles there was a sign designating the dirt road to the Williams Creek Fish Hatchery. The turnoff to Alchesay Fish Hatchery is about 10 miles farther on State 73. These hatcheries keep the streams and lakes on the reservation stocked with trout. Visitors can tour both facilities and, with tribal permits, fish reservation waters.

Between those turnoffs from State 73, off to the west, is the grave of Alchesay, the most revered of the White Mountain Apache chiefs. As a scout for the U.S. Army in the 1870s, he was awarded the Congressional Medal of Honor for his role in the battle of Turret Mountain — one of the campaigns against warring Apache tribes.

Right after the Alchesay Hatchery turnoff, the pines gave way to bushy junipers and other evergreens, and a large, smooth cliff protruded from a mountain. Near this point, the officially designated scenic drive ended, but we continued on to loop back to Pinetop rather than retrace the drive we had just made.

Within a few minutes we were entering the quiet town of Whiteriver, headquarters of the Fort Apache Reservation.

At the edge of town we came to a deep gorge and looked down to see the White River.

A few miles farther on State 73 we came to Fort Apache, located on a circular drive just off the highway to the left. Built at the confluence of the White River's east and north forks, the fort was established as Camp Ord by Major John Green on May 16, 1870. The name changed several times — Camp Mogollon, Camp Thomas, Camp Apache — before becoming Fort Apache on April 5, 1879. General Crook took command of the installation in 1871, organizing Indian scouts in several campaigns against hostile Indians, including the Tonto Basin Campaign (1872-73), Victorio (1879), and the Geronimo Campaign (1881-86).

In 1922, no longer needed for military purposes, the fort was converted to an Indian boarding school and named in honor of President Theodore Roosevelt.

We wandered into the Apache Cultural Center on the old post, walking past the elders who sat talking quietly on the porch. In a small alcove, newspaper clippings announced local events. A small, handwritten sign declared entrance to the center free, but noted there is a $5 charge to take pictures of the items inside. Throughout the center is an impressive display of traditional Apache attire, headdresses, tools and weaponry, foodstuffs, and housing examples. Portraits of great Apache leaders, such as Alchesay and Geronimo, hang throughout the small building. Videos depicting traditional native dances, farming techniques, and important ceremonies played on a VCR for a small group of visitors. We stopped to watch for a while.

There's no charge for taking pictures outside, and we wandered along the street with our camera, photographing several structures. General Crook's cabin, originally made of logs, was undergoing extensive renovation. Farther on, we saw a large, beautiful two-story stone house. Built around 1893, the house at one time served as the commanding officer's quarters. A small one-story house next to it housed several of the fort's officers. Today, some of the old houses are vacant and some are occupied.

Across the grounds, Indian children played near the

(OPPOSITE PAGE) *Sundown throws a red blanket over a stock tank near the Black River south of Whiteriver.* RANDY A. PRENTICE
(ABOVE) *The White River streams through Post Office Canyon alongside State Route 73 north of Fort Apache and Whiteriver.*

large school, as long, yellow school buses came and went along the dusty driveways. As we left, I pondered the mixing of old and new at Fort Apache.

To step even further back in time, you can obtain an "Other Activities" permit from the tribe and travel six miles west of Fort Apache to the Kinishba Ruins.

Kinishba is Apache for "brown house." On this site, Indians built two large pueblos and several small buildings between A.D. 1232 and 1320. Walk around the outside and imagine life as it must have been 750 years ago for the Indians who once thrived there.

The part of the drive actually designated as scenic runs just under 11 miles, from Hon-Dah to Whiteriver. But for a beautiful drive through spectacular cliffs and vistas, continue on around to Carrizo, then take State Route 60 north to State Route 260. Paved the whole way around, it's a pleasant trip, especially if you're staying in Show Low, Pinetop, or Lakeside. ⊠

## When You Go

**Reservation Permits:** Fishing, hunting, camping, picnicking, and all other recreational activities on the Fort Apache Indian Reservation require tribal permits. For detailed information and permits, call the Wildlife and Outdoor Recreation Division, 520-338-4385. For information only, call the Apache Tourism Office, 520-338-1230. They also can tell you which retailers can sell you permits.

**Nohwike Bagowa/Apache Culture Center:** Open Monday through Friday (8 a.m. to 5 p.m. in winter, 7:30 a.m. to 4:30 p.m. in summer) and some summer weekends. Fee. 520-338-4625.

**Kinishba Ruins:** From Whiteriver, go southwest six miles on State Route 73. A sign marks the turnoff to the right on a dirt road. Keep left at the fork. Ruins are two miles from the paved road. Obtain "Other Activities" permit.

**Apache-Sitgreaves National Forest, Lakeside Ranger District:** Provides brochures and maps for recreational opportunities. 520-368-5111, or TTY/hearing impaired, 520-368-5088.

**Lodging:**

Hon-Dah Resort-Casino-Conference Center; restaurant, mini-mart, RV park. Hon-Dah. 520-369-0299, or toll-free, 800-929-8744.

White Mountain Apache Motel; restaurant, gift shop. Whiteriver. 520-338-4927.

In the Show Low and Pinetop-Lakeside areas, two chambers of commerce can help you locate lodging and provide other information about White Mountains recreation:

**Pinetop-Lakeside Chamber of Commerce:** 674 E.. White Mountain Blvd., (P.O. Box 4220), Pinetop 85935. 520-367-4290.

**Show Low Regional Chamber of Commerce:** 951 W. Deuce of Clubs, Show Low 85901. 520-537-2326.

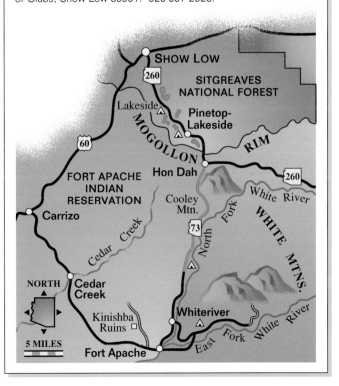

# White Mountain Scenic Road

On the second day of our White Mountains tour, we again drove southeast from Pinetop and Lakeside to the junction of state routes 260 and 73. The White Mountains Scenic Road begins on State Route 260, just east of Hon-Dah, which once was called Indian Pine. In the Apache language, Hon-Dah means "welcome" or "be my guest."

We sped right past the Hon-Dah casino, though we were tempted for a moment to go in and try our luck. But it was a glorious day to be outdoors. The tops of pines were brushing against the vivid, blue sky and aspens were glistening like gold-tinseled trees.

Just beyond Hon-Dah we came to the community of McNary. Set about 50 yards to the right of the highway was a shack and a home-made sign advertising Indian tacos — a pizza-like food consisting of fry bread topped with beans, onions, cheese, and green chile. It is delicious.

A few miles east of McNary, the highway cut through a bright green meadow. It stretched endlessly, rolling away from each side of the road and disappearing into forests on the horizons. Serenity spread over the meadow like a warm blanket, and we basked there alongside the highway, taking time to reflect on the beauty.

Resuming our drive, we soon overtook a bicyclist pedaling leisurely on the road, which seemed well-suited to a bicycling adventure.

Beyond the trees, several horses grazed in a large clearing, swishing long, thick tails lazily across their hocks. One raised his head to stare as we passed by.

Eleven miles east of Hon-Dah, we saw on the left the entrance to Big Bear Lake and Little Bear Lake (Shush-Be-Tou and Shush-Be-Zahze in Apache). Right after that, on the right, came State Route 473, the road to Hawley Lake, located about eight miles south of State 260. The complex around the 300-acre impoundment includes cabins, camping facilities, boat rentals, and a grocery store.

Continuing on State 260, I settled into a relaxed stupor when a stunningly bright field of red and gold aspens ignited the hillside on our right. The mountain rising in the background appeared to be ablaze as well. With that scene, I concentrated on focusing my attention on the landscape and we approached A-1 Lake, located just off the highway on the right.

We stopped to look around and stretch a bit. The wind and cool temperature made us shiver fiercely as we watched the fishermen. Some waded out into the water, while others stayed on the bank. I shook so hard my teeth chattered. After a few minutes we ran back to our sport

**Name:** White Mountain Scenic Road.

**Route:** A loop consisting of state routes 260, 273, and 261.

**Mileage:** 85 miles from Pinetop to Hon-Dah, Big Lake, Eagar, Springerville, and back to Pinetop.

**Time to allow:** Three to four hours.

**Elevation:** 7,500 feet at Hon-Dah; 9,100 feet at Big Lake; 7,000 feet at Eagar.

**Overview:** Another excellent choice for a fall colors drive, this loop cuts through the northeastern edge of the Fort Apache Indian Reservation and passes by several small trout lakes and the base of Mount Baldy, the tallest peak in the White Mountains. About 16 miles of the trip goes over an unpaved road that is suitable for a passenger vehicle, except in winter.

(OPPOSITE PAGE) *The Black River's Three Forks area lies southeast of the junction of state routes 273 and 261.* (ABOVE) *A fly fisherman finds solitude on the West Fork of the Black River.* BOTH BY RICHARD STRANGE (TOP) *Wild iris bloom along State Route 260 in the White Mountains, east of McNary.* JERRY JACKA

utility vehicle. Later, I learned that A-1 was the identification number that the Army had assigned to Alchesay, an Apache chief and Army scout who won the Congressional Medal of Honor.

Just beyond A-1 Lake, we turned right onto State Route 273, the road to Sunrise Park Resort, a ski, fishing, and recreation area owned and operated by the White Mountain Apache Tribe. Pulling over, I photographed a herd of cattle grazing in a field just across the road. Then I turned to stare at several odd, shiny metal panels on the other side of the road. I later was told that these billboard-looking devices are snow fences, installed to help stop blowing snow from piling up on roads.

Just beyond the Sunrise complex, there was a sign warning: "No winter maintenance November to May." At about the same point, we left reservation land and entered the Apache-Sitgreaves National Forest and pavement turned to gravel. The scenery jiggled a bit

(ABOVE) *Golden aspen trees glow in late afternoon light along the popular Big Lake in the White Mountains.* (RIGHT) *A meadow dotted by brown-eyed Susans glistens in Lee Valley. The adjacent forest has fir and spruce trees.* BOTH BY RANDY A. PRENTICE

now, but it seemed even more beautiful than that which we had seen from the paved road. It's amazing how much closer you feel to your surroundings when you're bouncing along in the dirt.

Mountain peaks poked up at several points south of us. The tallest, named Dzil Ligai, is sacred to the Apache people. Listed on maps as Mount Baldy, it is the central volcano in the White Mountains volcanic field. The field is composed of a central cluster of large stratovolcanoes, like Baldy, and more than 200 smaller cinder cones. The volcanic rock around 11,590-foot Mount Baldy may be as thick as 4,000 feet in places. Later on the drive we would pass through a rolling landscape filled with smaller volcanic cinder cones.

Soon we rolled onto pavement again and found ourselves on a narrow, one-lane bridge staring down at a tiny creek flowing through a small canyon.

Climbing slowly upward, I stared dreamily at the scenery as we wound around the switchbacks cutting through the trees. I might have tied a scarf around my head to keep my mouth from hanging open, but I didn't think of it then. Everything had such a mystical quality. I felt I had been transported into the setting of one of Grimm's fairy tales.

Towering blue spruce, white fir, and Douglas fir trees crowded the road's edges, while aspens shivered in between. Red, orange, and golden leaves swirled in flurries across the roadway in front of us as we crept along, trying not to disturb the silence. They fluttered this way and that, dancing at the roadsides, then flew suddenly upward and caught in the branches of taller trees.

By now, we had entered Lee Valley, but it could have been Heaven. The pavement ended again just before we turned toward Lee Valley Reservoir. Another sign declared that only fly and lure fishing were permissible at the 50-acre reservoir. We found a small, quiet lake with

deep, dark waters that rippled in the breeze — the same freezing wind we had encountered at the last lake, lucky us. The elevation here was about 9,400 feet.

As we strode across the gravel parking lot, an older gentleman shot us a lopsided grin, shrugged and shivered, jerking his head toward three children that cavorted in the parking lot. We smiled back and walked to the water's edge. I stuck my fingers in and pulled them out frozen. Glancing at the children who seemed so oblivious to the cold, we retreated to the warmth of our vehicle, and the thermos of hot coffee still stowed between the seats.

We headed out again along the main road, seeing several offshoots winding back into the mountains, all marked for four-wheel-drive vehicles only. Before long, State Route 273 joined State Route 261 at Crescent Lake. We went south (right) and in a mile or so were driving alongside Big Lake, viewing a most unusual sight — cattle and fishermen sharing the banks of the lake. Cattle and fishermen milled about, each wandering among the cars and trucks parked at the water's edge. Both animals and people seemed quite at ease with each other.

Chuck stepped from the truck to snap some pictures while I watched from inside. From what I remembered, he didn't have a lot of experience with large animals. Almost as one, the cattle began flicking their tails and

tossing their heads. Then, thrusting their noses upward, they startled into a trot, moving quickly along the bank toward the fishermen. Chuck hurried back, breathlessly laughing, "It's a stampede."

When the Big Lake visitor center and campgrounds are open, from about Memorial Day (May) through Labor Day (September), the rangers feature slide shows and nature walks. The lake also has a small store and a gas pump by the boat ramp; the vendor rents fishing boats and sells bait and other fishing gear until about late October or the first big snow — whichever comes first.

We made it around the bend in time to see a large, brown bull standing by the road, watching the cows and calves. He didn't look like one to be messed with.

We had to stop for a few minutes while a cowboy on horseback herded two young steers and a cow across the road in front of us, so we admired the smooth, golden plains that rolled by on either side. Chuck remarked how the landscape looked like Kansas. But just as I began

searching the skies for Dorothy's house, we were driving through another wooded area. We retraced our path back toward the junction of state routes 273 and 261 and continued north on 261 toward State Route 260.

As we passed Mexican Hay Lake, a weedy lake of some 150 acres with a brushy shoreline, the road began to curve and switch sharply, forcing us to slow our speed considerably. Practically crawling around one menacing turn, we found ourselves staring at an intriguing four-wheel-drive trail that all but disappeared into the mountainside. I was now driving, so I decided to see where the little trail went.

With our vehicle in four-wheel drive, we set off into the woods. It was exhilarating and frightening at the same time. We bounced and climbed over ruts and rocks, and I thought once we might tip. Yet once we decided to retreat, it seemed impossible to turn around. After countless times inching forward and back, forward and back, we finally did it.

If you have a four-wheel-drive vehicle, I recommend exploring these tiny backroads. You'll see nature in a way you simply can't from paved roads, and the way the blood races through your veins during these back-country jaunts is absolutely invigorating.

After we reached State Route 260, we decided to leave the officially designated scenic route and check out Eagar and Springerville, so we turned right.

Approaching Eagar, I wondered if we had somehow been transported into Vermont or maybe New Hampshire. Quaint little houses with pointed rooftops dotted the hillsides and valley, all surrounded by lush green pastures and picket fences. Everything nestled snugly beneath groves of bright red and green trees.

We returned to State 260 and headed west toward Pinetop. After

(LEFT) *Volcanoes left these dome-shaped rocks in the Mount Baldy Wilderness.* ROBERT G. McDONALD (OPPOSITE PAGE) *Mexican Hay Lake lies alongside State Route 261 in a broad valley.* GEORGE STOCKING

10 miles we passed State Route 373, which roams through a gentle valley and dead-ends in the resort village of Greer. Straddled along the Little Colorado River, Greer is popular with fishermen and other outdoor recreationists. Among the lodges in the village is one founded in the 1920s by Molly Butler, daughter of a pioneer who settled in Greer in the late 1880s.

Continuing west on State 260, the trees alongside the road gave way to a rolling sea of hills, cones and meadows. At about Milepost 389 we were entering yet another dimension of Arizona's landscape — the White Mountain volcanic field. Mount Baldy, ahead of us and to the left, is the central volcano in the field littered with characteristic cinder cones. Most of the cinder is covered by grass but a few cones have been opened and mined for material for blocks and paving.

We were in the volcanic field until we reached McNary, just a few miles from our base in Pinetop. ✍

## When You Go

**Apache-Sitgreaves National Forest:** Lakeside Ranger District, 520-368-5111, or TTY/hearing impaired, 520-368-5088; Springerville Ranger District, 520-333-4372 or TTY/hearing impaired, 520-333-6335. Available maps detail hiking, biking and horseback-riding trails, bird checklists, information on plants and wildlife in the area, and much more. Two especially helpful publications are "Recreational Opportunities on the Apache-Sitgreaves National Forests" and "Recreation Sites in Southwestern National Forests and Grasslands."

**Sunrise Park Resort:** 800-772-7669 or 520-735-7600.

**Reservation Permits:** Fishing, hunting, camping, picnicking, and all other recreational activities on the Fort Apache Indian Reservation require tribal permits. For detailed information and permits, call the Wildlife and Outdoor Recreation Division, 520-338-4385. For information only, call the Apache Tourism Office, 520-338-1230. They also can tell you which retailers can sell you permits.

*See listings for Coronado Trail and White River Scenic Road on pages 35 and 45.*

# Coronado Trail Scenic Road

**EASTERN**

I n 1540, Spanish explorer Francisco Vasquez de Coronado trekked through eastern Arizona's rugged terrain, searching for the Seven Cities of Cibola. His expedition followed the paths of ancient Indian traders north to the Zuni River and then turned east into what now is New Mexico. The route is said to have included what now is the Coronado Trail Scenic Road.

On a mid-September day, I gazed at stands of brilliantly-colored aspens quaking gently alongside the highway, and silently assumed that Coronado and his men were blinded by the fabled stories of gold in the seven cities. Otherwise, their journey likely would have ended here with the men on their knees, fervently praising this land where gold grows on trees.

On the north, the scenic drive designation begins just south of Springerville and Eagar. From there, we rolled south across a valley and then east onto a hill dotted with juniper and piñon pine and overlooking Springerville and the Little Colorado River.

About 10 miles from Springerville, we reached Nelson Reservoir stretching for a mile along the highway. The Apache-Sitgreaves National Forest recreation site includes a 60-acre lake stocked with rainbow, brown, and brook trout. There are picnic tables, restrooms, boat ramps, and handicap facilities, but no camping. Those who stop are treated to a beautiful view of rounded Escudilla Mountain to the southeast, a 10,955-foot ancient volcano. Escudilla is the Spanish word for soup bowl. That's what the mountain looks like — an upside-down bowl.

With the Escudilla Mountain Wilderness crowning the view, we continued south through another valley to Nutrioso, a town settled in the 1870s. The name is a combination of Spanish words meaning beaver and bear.

Three miles south of Nutrioso, we turned left from the Coronado Trail onto Forest Road 56, which leads east for about a half-hour to Terry Flat, the large meadow at the foot of the mountains, and the Escudilla

**Name:** Coronado Trail Scenic Road.

**Route:** U.S. 191 and U.S. 191/180.

**Mileage:** Springerville to Clifton and Morenci, 123 miles, with Nutrioso, Alpine, and Hannagan Meadow in between.

**Time to allow:** Four to six hours.

**Elevation:** 6,800 feet at Springerville, 8,000 feet at Alpine, 9,100 feet at Hannagan Meadow, 4,800 feet at Morenci.

**Overview:** This twisting drive begins in a grassy valley of the Little Colorado River; climbs the forested White Mountains; drops off the Mogollon Rim, the southern edge of the Colorado Plateau; passes a huge open pit copper mine; and ends north of the mining towns of Morenci and Clifton. At times, the road demands that you drive no faster than 10 or 15 miles an hour. The road is open all year, but you'll encounter snow in the winter.

Wilderness. Once grizzly bear territory, the 5,200-acre wilderness is now a hiker's and animal-watcher's heaven. Although the last grizzly in the area was killed more than 50 years ago, the area is home to black bears, elk, mule deer, weasels, Abert and red squirrels, wild turkeys, goshawks, mountain blue birds, hummingbirds — the list goes on.

If you want a hike, Escudilla National Recreation Trail forays through 3.3 miles of aspens, berry-bushes and forests of old-growth Engelmann spruce and Douglas and white fir. The trail leads from Terry Flat to Escudilla Lookout, Arizona's highest fire lookout tower.

I suppose a cautiously driven passenger car could make the trip, but we appreciated our high-clearance vehicle. If you make this side trip, allow at least 90 extra minutes.

Filled with a sense of serenity, we continued on the Coronado Trail and 17 miles south of the Terry Flat turnoff we passed Forest Route 249, which wends for some 20 miles though a valley to Big Lake, one of Arizona's most popular trout waters.

Slowly we made our way on U.S. 191 to Alpine. Named by Mormon settlers who founded the town in 1879, it was originally called Frisco for the nearby San

(OPPOSITE PAGE) *Viewed from Escudilla Mountain, the Coronado Trail snakes through the White Mountains just north of Alpine. Tal-Wi-Wi Lodge is visible at right.*
(ABOVE) *Hannagan Meadow's pastoral setting midway through the Coronado Trail trip makes it ideal for stretching cramped legs.*
BOTH BY JERRY JACKA

Francisco River. Later, they renamed it after deciding their mountains looked a lot like the Alps.

Fishing and hunting are excellent in and around Alpine, and there are numerous hiking, mountain biking, and horse riding trails. In the winter, you can enjoy cross-country skiing, sledding, snowmobiling, and ice fishing. If you are heading south, take note that Alpine offers the last chance for gasoline and groceries until Morenci, some 90 miles away.

The Blue Range Primitive Area lies just south of Alpine, a rugged wilderness divided by the south-flowing Blue River. The Mogollon Rim crosses the area from west to east, and there are rim trails located between mileposts 227 and 226. Geologic upheavals have created stunning rock formations and steep canyons.

Wildlife in the area includes Rocky Mountain elk, Coues white-tailed deer, javelina, black bear, mountain lion, and bobcat. There are also several varieties of rare birds such as the southern bald eagle, spotted owl, and olive warbler.

We wound lazily through the lush forests as mighty conifers towered above us. Often we caught glimpses of wildlife through the trees. There are some 460 curves and twists in the highway between Alpine and Morenci, definitely not a trip for those in a hurry. After crawling and twisting through a dense, isolated and incredibly beautiful stretch of forest for 22 miles, we saw the trees part like the Red Sea and Hannagan Meadow opened like a flower to the sun.

We pulled into Hannagan Meadow Lodge and sprang quickly from the car, glad to stretch our legs. A cool, fresh breeze wafted softly by, and I half expected tiny leprechauns to leap from the tall

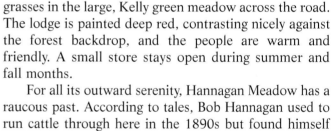

(ABOVE) *Terry Flat, an alpine meadow, flows out of Escudilla Mountain, north of Alpine.* JERRY JACKA
(BELOW) *Elk, like these in Hannagan Meadow, thrive in the White Mountains.*
(RIGHT) *The Phelps Dodge open-pit copper mine at Morenci is one of the world's largest.*
BOTH BY EDWARD McCAIN

grasses in the large, Kelly green meadow across the road. The lodge is painted deep red, contrasting nicely against the forest backdrop, and the people are warm and friendly. A small store stays open during summer and fall months.

For all its outward serenity, Hannagan Meadow has a raucous past. According to tales, Bob Hannagan used to run cattle through here in the 1890s but found himself indebted to a couple of locals to the tune of around $1,200. Bob either couldn't, or wouldn't, pay up, so his creditors chained him to a tree until relatives paid the debt in full. Once free, Hannagan departed the area rather hastily, but his name stuck around, although it's spelled in various ways.

Numerous hiking and mountain biking trails originate in Hannagan Meadow, and many lead into adjacent Blue Range Primitive Area.

Heading south again, we stopped at Blue Vista Overlook and Nature Trail, about seven miles south of Hannagan Meadow. The view is nothing short of stunning. We could see all the way to Mount Graham, the highest peak in the Pinaleno Range, some 70 miles to the southwest.

## When You Go

**Apache-Sitgreaves National Forest:** Springerville Ranger District, 520-333-4372 or TTY/hearing impaired, 520-333-6335. Alpine Ranger District, 520-339-4384. Clifton Ranger District, 520-687-1301.

**Little House Museum:** Fee. Photos and exhibits of pioneer life. Guided tour takes 90 minutes. About six miles west of Eagar on State 260 turn south onto County Route 4124, go about 2.5 miles and turn right at the fork. 520-333-2286.

**Casa Malpais:** Fee. Guided tour through ruins of an ancient pueblo takes about 90 minutes. Tour starts at museum, 318 E. Main Street, Springerville 85938. 520-333-5375. www.casamalpais.com

**Raven Site:** Fee. Guided tour through pueblo ruins takes about an hour. Open May to mid-October. Located about 12 miles north of Springerville off U.S. Route 191. 520-333-5857.

**Round Valley Chamber of Commerce:** 418 E. Main St. (U.S. 60), Springerville 85938. 520-333-2123.

**Greenlee County Chamber of Commerce:** 100 N. Coronado Blvd. (U.S. 191), Clifton 85533. Open 9 a.m. to 4 p.m., Monday through Friday. The chamber is located in a restored railroad depot, along with the local artists guild gallery. Ask about the historic district and the Greenlee Historical Museum. 520-865-3313.

**Phelps Dodge mine tour:** Free. Three-hour guided tour takes you into the world's second-largest open pit copper mine and other parts of the Morenci Mine operation. Call for tour times (limited availability) 520-865-1180 or, toll-free, 800-882-1291.

We resumed driving south at a snail's pace, every sharp curve and a nasty switchback reminding us that this was to be a slow drive all the way. The road's southern end descends rapidly, and soon the pine forests gave way to junipers, then desert scrub. Just after a sign noted the end of the Coronado Trail, the cliffs suddenly dropped off, revealing a most stunning unnatural wonder.

The Phelps Dodge Corporation's Morenci open pit mine gaped wide on our left — a huge, hungry mouth swallowing up the earth. Our emotions were unclear at first. Disdain followed surprise. Then came stubborn dislike. Finally, we grudgingly admitted that it was a spectacular sight, although a rude contrast from the natural wonders we had grown used to applauding. We stopped at the overlook long enough to marvel at the pit's incredible magnitude. Like the fascinated owner of a busy ant farm, I stared at the minuscule people driving tiny trucks far below. Then we drove downhill into Clifton.

At the bottom of the hill, legs wobbly, we clambered out at Clifton's restored railroad depot, grateful for public restrooms and a bubbling drinking fountain. ◤

# Swift Trail Parkway

## VENTURING UP A SKY ISLAND

When friends ask me what I like best about Arizona, I usually describe the diversity of the landscape — deserts and "sky island" mountains rising from them, high country lakes and streams, valleys and grassy meadows, rocky dells, and rocky and forested canyons. And the climate — in Arizona there are places where you can bask in 70-degree desert warmth and yet within two hours enjoy cold, snowy fun.

In a single drive, the Swift Trail Parkway encompasses all of these features. Rising from 3,200 feet, Swift Trail roams through the heart of the Pinaleno (also called Graham) Mountains, reaching its highest point at about 9,400 feet before dropping back down. In winter, you'll need a light sweater at the bottom and a heavy coat at the top.

Chuck and I started up the mountain one late-September afternoon. Initially, we drove over the desert floor, with ocotillos, barrel cactus, paloverdes, mesquites, hackberry, prickly pear, and cholla thickly spread among many other varieties of desert plant life.

By the time we reached Marijilda Canyon turnoff at 3.4 miles into the trip, we were entering a Sonoran Desert transition zone between scrublands and sloping grasslands. Views of the Graham Mountains filled the horizon ahead of us. Behind us sprawled the Gila Valley.

At 4.9 miles, we stopped to read plaques honoring the Jacobson family, whose members built a sawmill in this canyon now named after them, and Theodore T. Swift, for whom the trail was named.

A mile up the Swift Trail, a dirt road to the right goes one mile to Jacobson Overlook and a broad view of the Gila Valley.

Up another 1.5 miles, Angle Orchard, just off the Swift Trail on a road to the left, offers picnicking and hiking in the midst of thick oakland. The orchard operator sells apples and peaches in late summer and fall.

As we left the orchard we also left the last part of the highway that follows a fairly straight line. Now, a little less than 10 miles into the trip, switchbacks begin in earnest. Here you can enjoy striking views of the Gila

**Photographs by David W. Lazaroff**

**Name:** Swift Trail Parkway.

**Route:** State Route 366, which begins at U.S. Route 191 about seven miles south of Safford.

**Mileage:** 35 miles.

**Time to allow:** Four hours.

**Elevation:** Beginning at about 3,200 feet elevation, the route zigzags to about 9,400 feet, drops down to a flat, and ends just beyond a lake beneath 10,713-foot Mount Graham. In summer it's warm at the base and cool on high; winter temperatures are mild below and cold at the top. The upper portion of the road closes for the winter on Nov. 15 and opens on April 15 or later, as snow conditions permit.

**Overview:** Set your trip odometer to 0 at the junction of State 366 and U.S. 191 and begin to enjoy the only place in Arizona where you can readily drive a car so high up. Along the way, you'll enjoy broad vistas of valleys, rugged canyons, and seemingly endless mountainscapes with a variety of trees.

River Valley with an extra thrill — driving a road with virtually no shoulder, just a long, steep drop-off. You have entered pine country, and the first ones you'll see are Chiricahua pines.

By the time we reached Turkey Flat, 14 miles into the trip, we found ourselves surrounded by pine stands, tall grasses, and a myriad of wildflowers. In this area you'll notice several dirt roads leading off Swift Trail. They lead to more than 70 privately owned summer homes.

The Twilight Spring area begins at about mile 14.5, where a mile-long road leads to a camping area. This scenic stretch of the Swift Trail lasts for just over two of the drive's most beautiful miles. Steep slopes lined with white fir and pine trees flank the road. Sprinkled amid the trees and running along the edge of the highway are countless varieties of flowering shrubs, including the bright orange honeysuckle. Small streams run along the roadside during spring and summer.

Just beyond the 17th mile, picnic grounds and hiking trails appear at Ladybug Saddle. This place draws its name from the ladybugs that swarm here in the summer. We stopped to walk around, and I remembered what I had

(OPPOSITE PAGE) *Looking eastward from Mount Graham, near where the road pavement ends, sightseers can behold the broad San Simon Valley edged by the Whitlock Mountains.* LES MANEVITZ
(ABOVE) *A Douglas fir hosts these mushrooms.*

read about the bears that make their homes in the Pinalenos. There are signs posted at the picnic areas warning recreationists to keep coolers, picnic baskets, and other goody-containers locked in their cars.

Then, for some reason, I thought about the endangered twin-spotted rattlesnakes that also inhabit the area, and decided I would rather meet a bear. Fear is such an unreasonable thing.

A mile farther up the road we reached the south side of the Pinalenos and a panorama of the Sulphur Springs Valley and the Galiuro Mountains. Pines now dominated the slopes but there were thickets of red-gold aspens. Sheer cliffs rose majestically on one side, while rock outcroppings crowded us on the other.

Further on, just past mile 21, a small sign points the way to Snow Flat. We followed the narrow, dirt road about a mile back into the forest, where we found a grassy meadow and a pond. Picnicking and camping are allowed, but there are no facilities. A mile-long trail following a creek provides the perfect after-lunch hike to a small waterfall and stunning views of the valley below.

Or, you can drive less than a mile past the Snow Flat turnoff and stop at Shannon Campground, where there are restrooms, drinking water, and lots of great trails for hiking — or mountain biking, according to a couple of bikers just coming out of the woods. They blamed their heavy breathing on the high elevation, about 9,100 feet.

Remember the Marijilda Canyon turnoff at the start of the trip? At Shannon Campground you'll see Marijilda Creek, trickling its way down.

A steep dirt road leading from Shannon Campground climbs about two miles to Heliograph Lookout Tower. In 1886, during the final campaign against the Chiricahua Apaches, General Nelson Miles' troops kept a lookout from this peak and sent messages through a network of reflectors to forts and other troops.

That wasn't the only use the military found for the Pinalenos. Medics stationed at Fort Grant, at the base of the mountains, used the meadow now called Hospital Flat for a summer site where soldiers, wounded while fighting Apaches, could recuperate and escape the summer heat.

Today, camping and hiking are popular activities at Hospital Flat, located a little past mile 23. In the summer, colorful wildflowers fleck the meadow.

Before you get to Hospital Flat, the pavement ends at a gate. From here on, the road ahead is closed to motorized vehicles during the snow season between November 15 and approximately April 15. A road to the right is closed year-round to protect the Mount Graham red squirrel, a subspecies that lives only on this mountain. After a recent survey, Arizona wildlife specialists estimated there were no more than 350 Mount Graham red squirrels.

A little more than a mile from the gate there's a turnoff to Treasure Park. Legend has it that Mexican bandits buried stolen gold and silver here sometime before 1853 and they never returned for it. Except for that story, the site is unimproved, but you can camp or picnic here.

After that turnoff comes Hospital Flat. Next, Grant Creek flow from the dense pine forest, and runs along near the shoulder for about two miles. There are picnic areas near the creek.

The Hawk Peak waterfall, at about mile 28, sparkles like a jewel. This 30-foot waterfall spills over a series of rock outcroppings on Post Creek. Farther back from the road, the University of Arizona operates an astrophysical site.

At the Fort Grant overlook, not quite 30 miles into the trip, we were

(ABOVE) *Ladybugs find food and shelter in a corn lily leaf.*
(LEFT) *A mist covers Hospital Flat and the orange sneezeweed (a sunflower) highlighting the meadow.*
(OPPOSITE PAGE) *The Hawk Peak waterfall cascades for 30 or so feet.*

reminded just how high up we were — more than 9,300 feet. I was glad for the little rock wall that stood stubbornly between me and the dizzying valley far below.

A mile and a half farther up the road, the Columbine Work Center, a summer base for rangers, and Columbine Visitors Center, straddle the road.

After that, we passed Soldier Creek campground, which at 9,300 feet is the highest camping facility in the range. Beyond, we encountered a series of pretty meadows: Peters Flat, Chesley Flat, and Riggs Flat at mile 34.

Finally, we were at the end of the scenic drive. And what a welcome — the trash containers were all bear-proof, reminding me once again that the Pinalenos are reported to have the West's largest concentration of black bears. The flat, with an 11-acre lake stocked with trout, certainly was the busiest location on the mountain. So we put on our jackets and enjoyed the chilly weather and the view of the Aravaipa Valley and Galiuro Mountains miles beyond us.

The Swift Trail goes beyond Riggs Flats for a little more than a mile, to Clark Corrals, where there are two campsites, a toilet, corrals, a turn-around point, and the head of seven-mile Clark Peak Trail. But as it started getting dark, our minds turned again to those reinforced trash containers, and we decided to head back down. We stopped at the Fort Grant Lookout to watch the sunset. Holding hands there under the pink- and orange-streaked skies, with the first stars just beginning to twinkle overhead, I silently wished upon a star that all our journeys would be as lovely as this one. ⚑

# When You Go

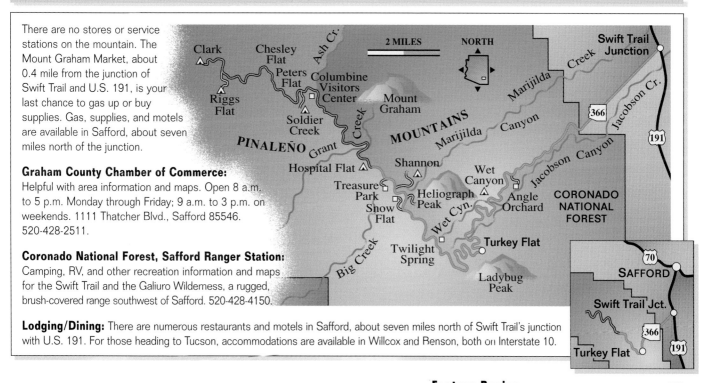

There are no stores or service stations on the mountain. The Mount Graham Market, about 0.4 mile from the junction of Swift Trail and U.S. 191, is your last chance to gas up or buy supplies. Gas, supplies, and motels are available in Safford, about seven miles north of the junction.

**Graham County Chamber of Commerce:** Helpful with area information and maps. Open 8 a.m. to 5 p.m. Monday through Friday; 9 a.m. to 3 p.m. on weekends. 1111 Thatcher Blvd., Safford 85546. 520-428-2511.

**Coronado National Forest, Safford Ranger Station:** Camping, RV, and other recreation information and maps for the Swift Trail and the Galiuro Wilderness, a rugged, brush-covered range southwest of Safford. 520-428-4150.

**Lodging/Dining:** There are numerous restaurants and motels in Safford, about seven miles north of Swift Trail's junction with U.S. 191. For those heading to Tucson, accommodations are available in Willcox and Benson, both on Interstate 10.

# Red Rock Scenic Road

**Editor's Note:** Five roads designated by the state of Arizona as scenic or historic center on Sedona, located at the base of the Mogollon Rim. Three of them stretch between Prescott and Sedona along State Alternate Route 89 (89A) — Mingus Mountain Scenic Road, Jerome-Clarkdale-Cottonwood Historic Road, and Dry Creek Scenic Road. They add up to a day's sight-seeing. The other two — Red Rock Scenic Road and Sedona-Oak Creek Canyon Scenic Road — also combine for an ideal day trip ending in Sedona.

Here is the travelogue for the Red Rock road:

**Name:** Red Rock Scenic Road.

**Route:** State Route 179 between Interstate 17's Exit 298 and Sedona.

**Mileage:** The exit is approximately 100 miles north of Phoenix and 45 miles south of Flagstaff. It's 15 miles from I-17 to Sedona.

**Time to allow:** One to two hours after you reach Exit 298.

**Elevation:** 3,600 to 6,000 feet.

**Overview:** Red Rock Scenic Road takes you up a valley dotted with rock formations chiseled by wind and water and colored by minerals. The formations — many of them are named — rise as much as 2,100 feet from the valley floor. Their colors — yellows, reds, browns, and oranges interspersed with evergreens — change as the sun and clouds move across the sky.

On a sunny August day, as we cruised off Interstate 17 onto State Route 179, I was gripped by a rush of excitement. Having made this trip many times before, I knew what lay ahead, just beyond the first few curves after the turnoff. But knowing only seemed to whet my appetite. My anticipation continued to mount as we followed the two-lane, serpentine road through vegetation consisting of juniper, piñon, and grasses.

"It should be anytime now," I predicted, glancing at Chuck, trying to mask my excitement.

"Okay," he answered, smiling, patting my knee.

As the road continued snaking, the landscape's red soil took on a crumbled appearance like flaky pie crust. Then, Bell Rock rose slowly from the horizon.

"There, look!" I shouted to Chuck, who stared at me with a mildly pained expression.

Towering over the valley, Bell Rock blazed against an azure sky. I gazed in awe across the distance, following the blanket of green to the base of the curiously eroded rock. Patches of shrubbery trailed up its sides in a quilt-like mix of color and texture.

Before long, stunning Cathedral Rock appeared on the horizon, beautifully draped in Southwestern colors. Other colorful rock formations popped up along the skyline, wearing deep purplish-reds or striped brown and tan, like the inside of a Snickers bar. Jutting skyward alongside

(OPPOSITE PAGE) *Sightseers behold Bell Rock as they travel north on State Route 179.* GEORGE STOCKING
(ABOVE) *Beaver Head Spring lies a quarter mile west of State Route 179 on Dry Beaver Creek about two miles north of I-17.* JERRY JACKA

several buttes were the fascinating rock sculptures called spires — thin, sandstone columns, smoothed and hardened by the elements over time.

It doesn't matter how many times I make this drive — I am awed each time by the beauty and the power of this land. As I peeked at Chuck, I couldn't resist the urge to smile. He was staring avidly out the window, just like me.

As I cruised along, I had no trouble understanding the scenic designation appointed to a 10-mile stretch of this road. Adjectives like magnificent, awe-inspiring, incredible, and beautiful seem to roll off the tongue.

Yet many people believe there is something else worth discovering in red rock country, the region incorporating Sedona and Oak Creek Canyon. New Age followers insist the area contains many vortexes, or "psychic-energy points" and have identified those, such as Bell Rock, which are said to energize and inspire visitors with their "electric energy." Others, like Cathedral Rock, are said to have a calming effect because of their "magnetic energy."

The origins of red rock country reach back some 330 million years, when an ocean covered the land below the Mogollon Rim. The waters receded, and swamps and flood plains formed. Later, another ocean filled the basin. It, too, receded, creating a coastal desert. Approximately seven million years ago, volcanic eruptions occurred sporadically.

They lasted about 200,000 years. Proof of these events is recorded in the different strata on the canyon walls, buttes, and spires of red rock country. The brilliant red and orange hues are the result of iron in the sandstone and limestone layers oxidizing (rusting) in the rain. And the artistic rock formations owe their shapes to varying hardness in each rock layer, a variance that allows layers to respond differently to water and wind.

We came to the Village of Oak Creek and Verde Valley School Road on the left. If you turn onto this road, just past Milepost 306, you will be treated to a brief drive offering splendid views of Bell Rock and other formations.

Two miles farther north on 179 you'll come to Bell Rock Vista Point, from which a trail leads to an ideal spot for taking pictures.

Man-made structures among such natural splendor might seem out of place, unless you're referring to the Chapel of the Holy Cross. I always start looking for it too soon along State 179, but my anticipation just makes the view that much better when I finally see the chapel rising out of Twin Buttes. A commanding structure, it manages to be at peace with its setting amid rocky buttes. From the chapel's parking lot you get a different perspective of Bell and Courthouse rocks.

Marguerite Brunswig Staude commissioned the design and construction of the chapel in 1953 as a memorial to her parents and called it "a spiritual fortress so charged with God that it spurs man's spirit godward!"

Staude's claim appears to apply as readily to the entire area as it does to the chapel. Red rock country is second only to the Grand Canyon as a tourist attraction in Arizona. Some visitors seek the beauty and excitement of the area; others search for spiritual peace.

Opportunities for enormous fun include various special events such as a jazz festival, shopping, hiking, camping, mountain biking, jeep tours, balloon and helicopter rides, horse riding, bird-watching, and photography. After passing several comfortable places to lodge, shop, and dine, we reached Sedona and Schnebly Hill Road. The road twists along the east wall of Oak Creek Canyon to

(LEFT) *A panorama of red rock cliffs delights travelers on State Route 179.* BOB & SUZANNE CLEMENZ
(ABOVE) *The Chapel of the Holy Cross blends with buttes between Oak Creek and Sedona.*
GEORGE STOCKING

## When You Go

**Sedona-Oak Creek Canyon Chamber of Commerce:** Provides detailed information on lodging, dining, and recreational opportunities. Located in Sedona on State Route 89A at Forest Road. 520-282-7722 or 800-288-7336.

**Chapel of the Holy Cross:** Turn east from State Route 179 onto Chapel Road about a half mile north of Milepost 310. The chapel is open for visitation daily, but no services are held there.

**Montezuma Castle National Monument:** Fee. For a side trip, turn east from I-17 at Exit 298. Signs will direct you to a preserved cliff dwelling built by Sinagua Indians in the 12th and 13th centuries. The monument includes Montezuma Well, a sink hole filled with blue-green water. A short trail leads you down to the point where the water goes into a hill to emerge on the other side in Beaver Creek. Allow two to three hours to tour the dwelling site and the well. 520-567-3322.

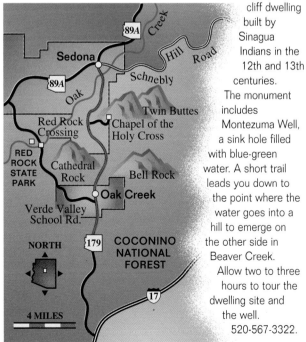

the top of the Mogollon Rim at an elevation of about 6,000 feet. There's a grand overlook about 6.5 miles up the road. From that vantage point you get an overview of the canyon and can see Mingus Mountain on the southwestern horizon hovering over Jerome.

The road was named for Carl Schnebly, who migrated to Oak Creek Canyon with his wife, Sedona, in 1902. The plush Los Abrigados resort stands today where the couple built their two-story, wood-frame house. And yes, the town is named for Sedona Schnebly.

We passed on by the dirt road, though. It's a lovely but forbidding path, even in good weather. It's best traveled in a high-clearance vehicle. On this day, we would have to remain on paved roads with our ground-hugging sports car.

We pulled into a convenience store just south of the "Y," the junction where State 179 and State 89A meet. Standing in the parking lot, we surveyed the line of cars that stretched as far as we could see in both directions, like ants on their way to a picnic. I hoped they weren't all headed to Grasshopper Point.

# Sedona-Oak Creek Canyon Scenic Road

**Photographs by Bob & Suzanne Clemenz**

Before driving the Sedona-Oak Creek Canyon Scenic Road, my children and I spent a wonderful December day trekking through Sedona and along Oak Creek. Even in summer the water in Oak Creek can numb you. When we stuck our fingers in the creek on this brisk day, it was positively bone-chilling. So we pursued land activities.

We began by browsing through the many shops, specialty boutiques, and art galleries lining both State Route 179 and State Route 89A. Along the way I learned that more than 300 artists — many nationally known — live in Sedona. Indeed, art has become a staple — as much Sedona as the famous red rocks themselves.

I am always especially impressed by the Mexican-styled Tlaquepaque, a maze of shops, galleries, restaurants, passageways, and courtyards with the feel of a Hispanic village laden with aged sycamores, fountains, potted plants, iron gates, and statues.

Sedona fudge from one of the shops garnered rave

**Name:** Sedona-Oak Creek Canyon Scenic Road.

**Route:** State Route 89A going north from Sedona.

**Mileage:** 30 miles round-trip from Sedona.

**Time to allow:** Two to three hours.

**Elevation:** 4,500 to 7,000 feet.

**Overview:** This road climbs between mileposts 375 and 390 so quickly that it traverses eight plant-life zones, ranging from desert grassland to riparian, oak woodland, piñon and juniper woodland, chaparral, and pine-fir forest. The tour makes an excellent drive for viewing autumn colors.

(OPPOSITE PAGE) *The brilliant autumn orange of maples intensifies the beauty of cliffs and vegetation along the West Fork of Oak Creek.*
(ABOVE, RIGHT) *Mild weather and dramatic scenery attract bicyclists to red rock country.*
(ABOVE) *A patio with bright red tulips and a fountain contribute to the Hispanic village aura of Tlaquepaque.*

reviews from all three of us, and I silently vowed to take a long hike to make up for my own indulgence. Michael, 9, gets enough exercise for 10 people in a normal day, and pushed hard for one of the jeep tours instead. Several companies offer thrilling jeep tours through red rock country. But on this day our goal was to drive up Oak Creek Canyon. So, I promised Mike we would return for a jeep tour without Kelsey who, at age 4, is hard to confine in a vehicle for too long.

Soon, we were on State Route 89A heading north to my all-time favorite spot, Grasshopper Point, a swim-hole getaway extraordinaire. It's a small, natural pool formed in a bend of Oak Creek. There used to be a tattered rope tied to a large tree overhanging the water, and my high school friends and I used to swing off into the icy depths. I smiled even as a tear threatened, remembering Shadow, my white shepherd, who used to follow me to the top of the lower cliff and jump with me into the freezing water below. Those were good times, yes.

Our next stop was Rainbow Trout Farm, another favorite of mine and the only place I've ever caught a fish. We arrived a few minutes after five o'clock — just after the gates had closed. Kelsey hopped about pathetically next to the creek, doing her I-can't-hold-it-much-longer dance, while I peered through the chain-link gate and wondered how I would find a rest room for her in time. Fortunately, a man finishing the day's chores spotted her antics and let us in. While Michael rushed her off, I explained about my book research. As it turned out,

the owner was on the premises, and Bill sent me off to talk to him, promising to take care of the kids. He said he had a little bait left over and that they could fish while he worked.

Dan Delaney, the owner, turned out to be a large, friendly man who took me for a tour. It had changed a lot since I had last been there. Dan remodeled extensively when he bought the farm three years ago, putting in walkways, barbecues, and tables. "I wanted it to be a nice place for families to come and fish, and then eat what they catch," he explained. The ponds and the incubating tubs are both stocked with natural artesian water from a spring on his property. His bottling company bottles water from another spring for his Purely Sedona label. As we walked along narrow boards over the runs where the young fish swim, protected by fences and net coverings, I asked if anyone had ever fallen in. He paused before saying, "Well, if you do, you'll be the first."

By the time we completed our tour of the property, Michael had caught two fish and Kelsey had one. Seeing their faces beam, I remembered what it felt like to catch my first fish. Dan wouldn't let me pay for the fish — but he did make me promise to take them home and eat them. "Just send me a copy of your book when it's done," he said as we parted ways. I decided I would personally bring it to him.

Slide Rock State Park was next on the agenda. Here, water enthusiasts will delight in experiencing Nature's own rock and water slide. You used to just walk around the guardrail and down to the slide, but now there's a well-maintained park with facilities and an entrance fee.

Wear old, denim shorts when you slide, because even though the rocks feel smooth and slippery, you'll wear out the thin fabric of a swimsuit in just a few passes. Believe me, that can be embarrassing. We walked in a ways and looked at the water slide, but the kids didn't even ask to give it a try. They had already felt the water.

We continued on up the highway toward Flagstaff, passing a pretty stone convenience store and the Junipine Inn. Here, the trees are mostly pines.

(OPPOSITE PAGE) *The camera condenses the four-mile expanse between Steamboat Rock (foreground) and Munds Mountain.*
ROBERT G. McDONALD
(LEFT) *The slippery chute in Oak Creek attracts endless numbers of fun lovers to Slide Rock State Park.*
(BELOW, LEFT) *Switchbacks continually confront drivers going up Oak Creek Canyon.*

## When You Go

**Sedona-Oak Creek Canyon Chamber of Commerce:** 520-282-7722 or 800-288-7336. *www.sedonachamber.com/*

**Slide Rock State Park:** On State 89A about seven miles north of town. Grasshopper Point is about two miles north of town on 89A; call Slide Rock State Park for information. 520-282-3034.

**Rainbow Trout Farm:** About three miles north of town on 89A. Fee. You can fish, no license required, and tackle is furnished. If you like, grill and eat your catch at the picnic area. 520-282-5799.

**Coconino National Forest, Sedona District:** Maps and information on campgrounds, hiking trails, and other outdoor recreation. 520-282-4119.

**Sedona annual events:** International Film Festival, March. Sedona Chamber Music Festival, May. Astronomy Festival, June. Jazz on the Rocks, September. Sedona Arts Festival, October. For details, check with the chamber of commerce or go online with the Arizona Office of Tourism, *www.arizonaguide.com/sedona/*

***Sedona Calling:*** This guide to sights and outdoor fun in Sedona's red rock country features scores of color photos and text detailing the history and charm of Sedona, neighboring Jerome, Verde Valley, and Oak Creek Canyon. Published by *Arizona Highways.* To order, call 800-543-5432 or 602-712-2000.

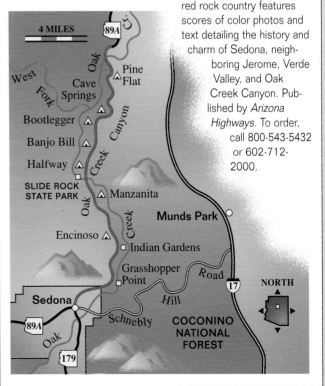

The scenic drive ends about 15 miles before you reach the top of the Mogollon Rim and Flagstaff (the scenic part doesn't end but the designation does) and although I wanted to go all the way, a snowstorm was threatening Flagstaff, and the kids wanted to get their fish home. So we turned around and headed back to Sedona, smelling the crisp air, the pines, the creek, and smoke from fireplaces. Warm lights shone in the windows, and in the shadowy distance, the buttes loomed over it all. As we piled out of the car at a restaurant just south of the "Y," I turned to stare at a nearby cliff, glowing bluish-white in the moonlight. And yes, I think I felt a tingle. ◪

# Mingus Mountain Scenic Road

**Photographs by George H.H. Huey**

Sitting practically on the ground in my black sports car, I gripped the steering wheel and waited, certain I had felt an almost imperceptible lurch. Yes, there it was again. The wind was actually shaking us. Usually, gales just skirt right over the top of this car, like it's not even there. But not this time.

"I'm hungry," came Kelsey's plaintive wail, for the hundredth time.

I don't know which is worse, freezing or starving, but I was willing to give starvation a try. Parked at a pull-out on State Route 89A near Granite Dells, I fetched our picnic lunch from the car trunk. Although Granite Dells provides ideal picnic sites, the weather this day dictated we would lunch in the car.

We had left Phoenix that December morning under warm, sunny skies, to head north and then west through Prescott Valley, Dewey, and now Prescott. Our aim was Mingus Mountain, the mountainside mining town of Jerome, and a trip to Sedona via its "back door."

State Route 89A wandered into a large, prairie-like valley. Lonesome Valley, I later learned. We left the shadows of the Bradshaw Mountains to strike out across the valley. Golden fields stretched widely and rolled gently toward Mingus and Hickey mountains ahead of us in the Black Hills range.

Milepost 332 signals the beginning of the Mingus Mountain Scenic Road. From there, 89A begins winding upward into the mountains, and the plains and Great Basin grasslands rapidly give way to forest dominated by ponderosa pines. For a while, I noticed oaks and junipers along the

**Name:** Mingus Mountain Scenic Road.

**Route:** State Alternate Route 89 (89A). At Exit 262 (Cordes Junction) on Interstate 17 go west on State Route 69 to Prescott and State Route 89. Go north on 89 for about five miles and turn right onto 89A.

**Mileage:** 68 miles from Phoenix to Cordes Junction; 34 more miles to Prescott; 33 more miles to Jerome.

**Time to allow:** Two to three hours from Exit 262 to Jerome.

**Elevation:** 5,354 feet at Prescott; 7,743 feet atop Mingus Mountain; 5,435 feet at Jerome.

**Overview:** This drive is the first leg on the "back door" road to Sedona. From mile-high Prescott, you'll pass by the rounded boulders strewn over Granite Dells, cross a prairie, and climb from piñon-juniper forest to pine country. Before you descend the steep west slope of 7,743-foot Mingus Mountain, you'll enjoy panoramic views of red rock country, San Francisco Peaks, and the Verde Valley.

(OPPOSITE PAGE) *Looking southward from Mingus Mountain, viewers can see the foreboding tones that inspired the naming of the Black Hills in what now is the Prescott National Forest.*
(ABOVE, RIGHT) *A seemingly unlikely mingling of agave and pine needles appears in the Mingus Mountain Recreation Area.*
(RIGHT) *Massive, dome-shaped rocks and cottonwood characterize the Granite Dells area near Prescott.*

road's edge, but they disappeared as we passed through Haywood Canyon.

We pulled into a scenic overlook (just before Milepost 337) and caught our first glimpses of the red rocks along the southern edge of the Colorado Plateau, the Mogollon Rim, and the Verde Valley. Potato Patch Campground and Mingus Mountain Recreation Area are close by for those who wish to camp, hike, ride mountain bikes, and explore. Mingus Recreation area is especially popular with hang gliders.

About two miles up the road is one of the most beautiful panoramic views I've seen, providing a combination of land and vegetative features seldom seen all at once. Conifer woodlands, semi-desert grasslands, river valleys, plateaus, and mountains sprawled below us. The San Francisco Peaks rose in the distance above the red rocks of the Mogollon Rim, and we had an extensive look at the Verde Valley this time.

Passing through Walnut Springs, we came next upon the Verde Central Shaft, offering up-close views of mine tailings, a rarity so close to the road. Then beautiful Hull Canyon, with its magnificent views of the Colorado Plateau.

Too soon, we rounded a bend and passed a sign signaling the end of our scenic route. The kids relaxed back into their seats, and even Michael seemed impressed, quite an accomplishment these days. Then Kelsey asked what was next, and Michael asked where Jerome was, and before I could answer, another bend produced another sign and *voila!*, we'd begun the next leg of our journey — the Jerome-Clarkdale-Cottonwood Historic Road. ✇

(OPPOSITE PAGE) *West of Mingus Mountain, the virtually treeless Lonesome Valley stretches toward Prescott and Granite Mountain. Bear grass, prickly pear cactus, and junipers indicate a transition vegetation zone.*
(ABOVE) *A thunderhead hovers over the Verde River Valley at Hull Canyon along State Route 89A.*

# When You Go

**Prescott National Forest, Prescott District:** Maps, information on hiking, camping, and other recreational opportunities. 344 S. Cortez, Prescott 86303. 520-771-4700 or, TTY (hearing impaired), 520-771-4708. *www.fs.fed.us/r3/prescott/*

**Prescott Chamber Tourist Information Center:** 117 W. Goodwin, Prescott 86302. 520-445-2000 or 800-266-7534. *www.prescott.org/*

**Prescott Valley Chamber of Commerce:** 809A E. State Route 69, Suite B, Prescott Valley 86314. 520-772-8857.

**Sunset Point Rest Area:** Offers expansive view of the Bradshaw Mountains and Black Canyon. Full facilities, vending machines. Interstate 17, Exit 252, about 55 miles north of Phoenix.

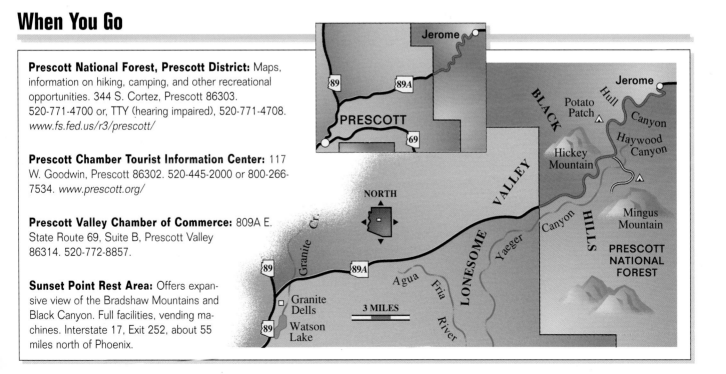

# Jerome - Cottonwood Historic Road

**Photographs by George H.H. Huey**

**Name:** Jerome-Clarkdale-Cottonwood Historic Road.

**Route:** State Alternate Route 89 (89A).

**Mileage:** 10.5 miles.

**Time to allow:** Two to three hours.

**Elevation:** 5,435 feet at Jerome.

**Overview:** This route, adjacent to the Mingus Mountain Scenic Road, celebrates three towns — Jerome, Clarkdale, and Cottonwood — that helped define Arizona's raucous youth. Along and near the officially designated route are museums, shops and galleries, historic parks, remains of ancient Indian dwellings, and the Verde River Valley.

The steep, twisting road up Cleopatra Hill on State Alternate Route 89 (89A) does not endear itself to the faint-hearted. After negotiating a narrow strip given to tight corners, blind curves, and slippery shoulders, drivers must catapult their vehicles up over a final hill to get onto Main Street. The drive makes a fitting entry into Jerome because there was nothing faint-hearted about this rowdy mining town that became a ghost town and resurrected as an artists colony and tourist attraction.

Jerome clings to the eastern side of Cleopatra Hill, a mountain so rich in copper, silver, gold, and other ores that it was called a "freak of nature" and a "veritable treasure trove" by Arizona historian Marshall Trimble. Here, atop Jerome, take a few moments to revel in the views of the Verde River Valley below and red rock country and the Peaks at Flagstaff to the north.

The town was named for Eugene Jerome, a New York financier and cousin of Jennie Jerome (the mother of Sir Winston Churchill). In the 1880s, Jerome financially backed a mining operation that became the United Verde. In 1888, Jerome sold the town and mining claims to Montana copper king William Andrews Clark.

In 1892, Clark built a narrow gauge railroad into Jerome from Chino Valley. The only other path into or out of Jerome was a treacherous wagon road leading through Yaeger Canyon. Throughout the 1890s, the United Verde Mine paid Clark dividends of over $3.5 million dollars per year. Before the mine shut down in 1953, Jerome was nicknamed the "billion dollar copper camp."

Building the town on such hilly terrain represented quite an architectural challenge. The result bears a striking resemblance to the Sinagua cliff dwellings built by the previous Verde Valley inhabitants. Main Street contorts in an agonizing fashion, attempting to dodge back and forth across the face of the mountain. Buildings balance precariously on flattened pads held in place by retaining walls, or are simply wedged into the hillside on grades of 20 to 30 percent. Roads sprout in all directions toward clusters of weathered wooden homes. Viewed from below, the whole place appears like a maze, a conglomeration of shapes, textures, levels, and retaining walls on edges of building pads.

Buildings along Main Street, whether masonry or wood, seem to have grown together, unified in appearance by age. Although Jerome owes its early existence to mining, it now has a reputation as an artists colony, and tourism helps fire the local economy. On any weekend,

(OPPOSITE PAGE) *Buildings cling to the 25-percent grade of Cleopatra Hill in Jerome, once a rowdy mining town and now an enclave for artists and craft workers.*
(TOP) *Nearly a thousand years ago, Sinagua Indians lived in a village now preserved as Tuzigoot National Monument. Mingus Mountain rises in the background.*
(ABOVE) *Streets in Jerome retain a 19th-century flavor.*

out-of-towners crawl all over Jerome, enjoying the various shops, art galleries, boutiques, and restaurants.

The kids and I browsed through several stores, including Skyfire, which sells a menagerie of household items, art pieces, T-shirts, and other souvenirs. We bought some glow-in-the-dark stars, resisting the urge to purchase an entire glow-in-the-dark galaxy. Nearby, The Copper Shop peddles copper jewelry and kitchenware, and there's an ice cream store nestled conveniently along the strip.

In conjunction with the National Trust for Historic Preservation, the Jerome Historical Society, which helped revive Jerome in the 1970s, has placed plaques on many of the buildings, explaining their significance.

But only one-third, about 300, of Jerome's original structures remain. Flames swept through town regularly because of cramped conditions and lack of water. Major fires struck the town every year from 1897 to 1899, and in 1915 the acclaimed Montana Hotel burned to the ground.

(LEFT) *Visitors can tour the Douglas Mansion, now operated as Jerome State Historic Park. The mansion was built in the days when copper mining generated enormous wealth in Jerome.*

(BELOW) *Two miles east of Clarkdale, Tuzigoot gives testimony that an ancient culture thrived in the area.*

(RIGHT) *The Verde Canyon Railroad runs along the banks of the Verde River between Clarkdale and Perkinsville.*

(FOLLOWING PANEL, PAGE 66) *A downed cottonwood tree provides a natural frame for the Verde River as it flows through Dead Horse Ranch State Park.*

During those years, Jerome was populated mainly by miners, most of whom spent their nonworking time boozing and visiting town brothels. Prostitution was legal at various times, and the "working girls" reported biweekly for required medical exams. Many religious zealots claimed God was using fire to wipe out Arizona's Sodom and Gomorrah.

Today, numerous historic structures remain in Jerome. They include the Douglas Mansion (now the Jerome State Historic Park) and the Powderbox Church (now privately owned), built by Mexican immigrant Sabino Gonzalez, who arrived in Jerome in 1926. This landmark is nicknamed the "Powderbox Church" because Gonzalez paid town youngsters a penny for each wooden blasting-powder box that they tore apart to supply him with boards for building the church. The first service — Methodist — was held there in 1941.

There are several restaurants and one-of-a-kind eateries in Jerome, including the Flatiron Cafe and the Jerome Brewery, which is housed in the old firehouse.

There's a ghost town at the edge of Jerome, and for a reasonable admission price visitors can see what an old mining town might have looked like. The Old Mingus Art Center in the lower part of town is also worth a look.

Clarkdale reposes quietly in the valley at the bottom of the hill along 89A. Originally built by William Andrews Clark in 1914 as a smelter town for the United Verde Mine, the town suffered economically once the mines closed.

Clarkdale is listed on the National Register of Historic Sites as a model planned community or company town. Clark apparently built the kind of homes his workers wanted, and rented them on company terms. He also built schools, parks, and apartments. Clarkdale was reportedly built at a cost of $1 million.

While in Clarkdale, look for the old Bank of Arizona building on Main Street to find the Clarkdale Antique Emporium and Soda Fountain. Owners Cindy and Dale Rogers not only carry American and European antiques and collectibles, but they run a truly old-fashioned ice cream parlor, complete with a 1920s soda fountain and rootbeer that they make themselves. Or take a leisurely ride on the Verde Canyon Railroad from Clarkdale through the remote upper canyon to Perkinsville. The train rolls along at a leisurely 12 miles per hour, 20 feet above the river, allowing sightseers an opportunity to glimpse the unspoiled habitat in the canyon. Watch for the blue herons flying above the water near Perkinsville.

Near Clarkdale you'll find Tuzigoot National Monument, a famous Sinagua village that sprawled over a hillside between A.D. 1125 and 1400. The structure had 77 ground-floor rooms, was two stories in most places, but had only one ground-level floor when Indians abandoned it. Inhabitants used ladders to reach roof hatches, then pulled the ladders in behind them. Evidence of earlier Hohokam dwellings exists in the area.

Just south of Clarkdale, at the junction of state routes 89A and 260, Cottonwood retains the Old Town District in the vicinity of Broadway (the road between Clarkdale and Cottonwood) and Main. The district provides the flavor of a bygone era.

Just off 10th Street, Dead Horse Ranch State Park is a 300-acre oasis along the Verde River. The park offers 67 campsites — many with water and electricity — RV hookups and hot showers. A well-stocked fishing lagoon keeps fishermen busy year-round.

After touring Cottonwood you are in position to start the final leg of the back door trip to Sedona — the Dry Creek Scenic Road.

# When You Go

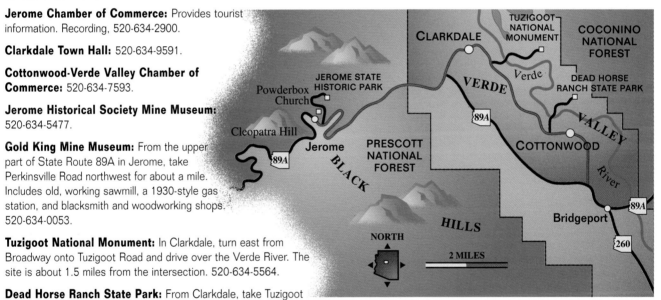

**Jerome Chamber of Commerce:** Provides tourist information. Recording, 520-634-2900.

**Clarkdale Town Hall:** 520-634-9591.

**Cottonwood-Verde Valley Chamber of Commerce:** 520-634-7593.

**Jerome Historical Society Mine Museum:** 520-634-5477.

**Gold King Mine Museum:** From the upper part of State Route 89A in Jerome, take Perkinsville Road northwest for about a mile. Includes old, working sawmill, a 1930-style gas station, and blacksmith and woodworking shops. 520-634-0053.

**Tuzigoot National Monument:** In Clarkdale, turn east from Broadway onto Tuzigoot Road and drive over the Verde River. The site is about 1.5 miles from the intersection. 520-634-5564.

**Dead Horse Ranch State Park:** From Clarkdale, take Tuzigoot Road to 5th Street and turn south. From Cottonwood, take 89A (Cottonwood Street) to Main Street, which makes a 90-degree turn to the left after you cross Mingus Avenue. From Main, turn right onto 10th Street, cross the Verde River, and drive about a mile to the park. 520-634-5283.

**Jerome State Historic Park:** In Jerome off 89A. 520-634-5381.

**Sycamore Canyon Wilderness:** Only hikers and horse riders allowed. Excellent hiking, camping, and scenic viewing. From Clarkdale, take Tuzigoot Road east; turn left after crossing the Verde River; trailhead is 10.5 miles ahead on a dirt road. Passenger cars with good clearance may attempt the drive. Call Sedona ranger station for wilderness information, 520-282-4119.

**Verde Canyon Railroad:** 520-639-0010 or 800-293-RAIL.

**Lodging and Food:** For more Jerome business listings, go online to www.jeromechamber.com/. For more Clarkdale business listings, see www.clarkdalechamber.com/. For more Old Town Cottonwood businesses, see www.oldtown.org/.

Ghost City Inn Bed & Breakfast, Jerome. 520-634-4678.

Jerome View Inn, 520-639-2824.

Sundial Motel, Old Town Cottonwood, 520-634-8031.

Flatiron Cafe, Jerome. 520-634-2733.

Jerome Brewery. 520-639-8477.

Clarkdale Antique Emporium & Soda Fountain. 520-634-2828.

Sossa's Deli & Verde Lea Market, Old Town Cottonwood. 520-634-8731.

# Dry Creek Scenic Road

**Photographs by Robert G. McDonald**

**Name:** Dry Creek Scenic Road.

**Route:** State Route 89A.

**Mileage:** 25 miles, Cottonwood to Sedona via Red Rock Loop Road.

**Time to allow:** One to two hours.

**Elevation:** 3,500 to 4,300 feet.

**Overview:** Starting just outside Cottonwood, this drive rolls through desert landscape into red rock country and Sedona. En route, you'll have the options of taking the Red Rock Loop Road or going up Dry Creek Road into an area that includes Boynton Canyon, Fay Canyon Arch, Devil's Bridge, Vultee Arch and Palatki, ancient cliff dwellings occupied by people of the Sinagua culture.

Just outside Cottonwood, State Route 89A winds northeast toward Sedona, home of artists, New Age believers and, of course, red rocks. The route's designation as Dry Creek Scenic Road begins about 10 miles from Cottonwood, between mileposts 363 and 364 amid rolling hills with mesquite and juniper trees and bunch grasses.

As we rolled through the desert landscape, we topped the ridge at White Flat, about a half mile past Milepost 364, and we caught our first teasing glimpse of red rock country in the distance straight ahead of us. Panoramic views featuring red buttes and spires silhouetted against the Colorado Plateau spread out before us, and I couldn't resist resting my foot just a little bit harder against the gas pedal. Dry Creek Scenic Road offers you the chance to watch these famous rock sculptures appear on the far horizon, and grow larger as you approach Sedona.

The countryside for the most part lies within the Coconino National Forest and has remained untamed. Dark, dense evergreens contrast vividly against the rich, red soil to create striking visual patterns. The highway's gentle slopes and curves provide quick glimpses of red and white sandstone cliffs in the distance, especially when passing over Dry Creek Bridge.

Just after the bridge lies the suburban community of Sedona Shadows, which includes a fire station and Sedona Hills Resort. The long Italian cypress hedgerow near the resort reminded me of my mother, who had a particular fondness for Italian cypresses and planted them at every house we lived in.

The terrain diversifies as you leave the Dry Creek area and continue on toward Sedona. Vegetation cover, consisting mostly of juniper and ponderosa pines, becomes more dense, and Scheurman Mountain now dominates the view. Windmill Mountain and a lone, red spire are visible on the distant horizon.

Lower Red Rock Loop Road intersects with the highway at Scheurman Mountain. Turn right here (just past Milepost 368), and Red Rock State Park is three miles up

(OPPOSITE PAGE) *Blooming century plants seem to stand as sentinels west of Dry Creek Road as sunset intensifies the color of sandstone buttes.*
(ABOVE) *Owl clover and red rocks make a picturesque scene.*
(RIGHT) *Magnificent red rock country lies ahead on Dry Creek Road.* BOB & SUZANNE CLEMENZ

the road. Even before you get to the park you get a fine view of Cathedral Rock. At the park, there's a visitors center, picnic area, and plenty of short hiking trails. Birding is good, and at least 150 species are documented in the area, so ask for the list if you're interested.

Red Rock Crossing can also be reached by continuing for about 4.5 miles northeast on Lower Red Rock Loop Road, which eventually becomes Upper Red Rock Loop Road. Two and a half of those miles are bumpy dirt road. At this point, Michael reminded me again that we needed to get a truck.

By the time you reach Upper Red Rock Loop Drive, spectacular views of the red rocks are dominant, close up and on the horizon. Besides Cathedral Rock, the Cockscomb formation, Chimney Rock, Capitol Butte, and Munds Mountain stand out.

The loop road returns to State Route 89A at about Milepost 370. Turn right, and in about a mile you will come to the paved Dry Creek Road. If you have time for a side trip, turn left. First thing, you will see the domed Capitol Butte off in the distance on your right.

A mile into Dry Creek Road you will come to Chimney Rock on the right and the Cockscomb formation on the left. In another mile, Dry Creek Road (also named Forest Route 152C) intersects with Forest Route 152, a dirt road that in less than 1.5 miles takes you to a parking area and a trail to Devil's Bridge. It's about an hour's hike to the natural arch. If you continue four more miles

to the end of the dirt road you will come to a trail that in an hour's hike comes to Vultee Arch.

Forest Route 152C continues on from its junction with 152. In less than a mile, 152C bears left at a Y junction. The road to the right (152D) goes into Long Canyon. By staying on 152C for four more miles you will come to Forest Route 525. Turn right and in a few hundred yards bear right onto Forest Route 795. This road (about two miles) leads to Palatki, an area with cliff dwellings and rock art left by Sinagua people who occupied the canyon between A.D. 1100 and 1300. Easily-followed trails lead from the parking area to the dwellings and red cliffs decorated with rock art.

Retrace your drive and turn left on 89A, pass through Grasshopper Flat into West Sedona, and you've made it in through the back door. 🔼

## When You Go

**Page Springs Hatchery:** Between mileposts 361 and 362 on State Route 89A, about eight miles north of Cottonwood. Visitors welcome. Operated by the Arizona Game and Fish Department, it's open 7 a.m. to 4 p.m., seven days a week. 520-634-4805.

**Coconino National Forest, Sedona:** Has information and maps for hiking and back country travel. 520-282-4119.

**Red Rock State Park:** Open daily for day-use only, no pets allowed. 520-282-6907.

**Sedona-Oak Creek Canyon Chamber of Commerce:** Call for information on accommodations and local events. 520-282-7722 or 800-288-7336. www.sedonachamber.com

(OPPOSITE PAGE) *Sunlight casts a fiery glow on the canyon wall above the ancient village of Palatki.*
(ABOVE) *Sinaguan people adorned canyon walls at Palatki with rock art. An easily-walked trail leads along the base of the canyon wall to dwelling ruins and the art.*

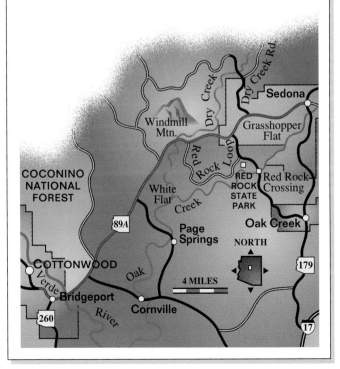

# San Francisco Peaks Scenic Road

When you live in the desert like I do, there's always something refreshing about a trip to the high country of the Colorado Plateau. It's as though my whole body, even my soul, prepares to really breathe again in the cooler air of northern Arizona.

So it was with particular zest that I scooted everyone into the car early one morning. We sped north up Interstate 17 from Phoenix toward Flagstaff, leaving the dry heat behind and setting our sights first on cool Flagstaff and its San Francisco Peaks.

The San Francisco Peaks may sound like a whole mountain range, but really they are three summits of one single, extinct volcano thrusting up among the smaller cinder cones and lava flows of the San Francisco Volcanic Field. Some geologists even refer to this dormant volcano as San Francisco Mountain, in singular terms rather than plural. The Peaks — Fremont, Agassiz, and Humphreys (at 12,643 feet Humphreys is Arizona's highest point) — are the eroded rim of the ancient volcano's crater.

As we drove into Flagstaff, we got a good look at these stony remnants of a prehistoric past rising above a modern city with pioneer roots. Rather than having to exit the freeway, drivers can take I-17 straight into town, where it becomes Milton Road near the Northern Arizona University campus.

We drove past Mars Hill, so I pointed out Lowell Observatory to the kids, where astronomer Clyde Tombaugh discovered the planet Pluto in 1930.

We headed roughly north on Milton, crossed under the railroad overpass, and rounded a curve, putting us briefly on Santa Fe Avenue/U.S. Route 66 before we turned left onto Humphreys Street. Then we turned left onto Fort Valley Road, which is also U.S. Route 180, on which lies the San Francisco Peaks Scenic Road.

U.S. 180 remains one of the principal roads to the Grand Canyon. Before 1900, there was no railroad service to the Canyon, and the Grand Canyon Stage Line operated from Flagstaff from 1892 to 1901. Although the

**Name:** San Francisco Peaks Scenic Road.

**Route:** U.S. Route 180 northwest from Flagstaff to State Route 64 at Valle Junction. From there, take 64 north to the Grand Canyon and east to Cameron. Then, U.S. Route 89 south to Flagstaff.

**Mileage:** The portion designated as a scenic road is 31 miles of U.S. 180. The entire loop is 190 miles.

**Time to allow:** Six to eight hours.

**Elevation:** 6,900 feet at Flagstaff and the South Rim of the Grand Canyon; 4,200 feet at Cameron.

**Overview:** This loop drive takes you through mountain meadows colored by grasses and wildflowers and into pine and aspen forests before swinging along the South Rim of the Grand Canyon. On the return to Flagstaff you pass by an immense gorge of the Little Colorado River and a portion of the Navajo Indian Reservation.

(OPPOSITE PAGE) *Meadows flank much of U.S. Route 180, spreading like an apron from the San Francisco Peaks.* (ABOVE) *Ponderosa pine trees develop massive, straight trunks.* BOTH BY ROBERT G. McDONALD
(RIGHT) *Lowell Observatory was built in the 1890s, when Earth and Mars came relatively close. The site became known as Mars Hill.* DON B. STEVENSON

main stage line ran east of the Peaks, an alternate route ran on the west side near present-day Hart Prairie.

The suburban homes got fewer as we neared Fort Valley Meadow. In the late 1800s, settlement in Fort Valley started near Leroux Springs as a timber camp, a source of railroad ties for the coming Atlantic and Pacific Railroad. The camp later was fortified into a stockade when Apache raids were feared.

Of course, along U.S. 180 the mountain remains the dominant, inescapable feature. In 1629 Franciscan friars established a mission at the Hopi village of Oraibi, nearly 100 miles northeast of the Peaks, and named them for St. Francis of Assisi. Early Spanish explorers had a less comforting name for these mountains — "Sierra Sin Aguas" or "mountains without water" because there are mountain springs but no permanent streams on the Peaks.

The Hopis, living on the mesas of northeast Arizona, knew and named the Peaks long before the friars and explorers came. The Hopi name "Nuva-teekiaovi" means "the place of snow on the very top." Here, they believe, is a sacred home of their deities, the supernatural Kachinas. Today, the Kachina Peaks Wilderness protects approximately 18,000 acres of the Peaks while respecting the mountain's religious importance to the Hopi.

Rolling green meadows, also called "parks," line the roadway. Brightly colored wildflowers quivered in the grass, touched by a cool breeze. Farther back across the fields, tall pines thickly swathed the Peaks from the base up the slopes. From the right viewpoint, you can pick out the bare ski runs of Snowbowl, Arizona's most centrally located snow skiing haven.

About seven miles out of Flagstaff we passed the entrance to the Snowbowl as the highway wound into a forest of thickly clustered aspens and ponderosa pines. The trees hugged together so tightly that I could imagine a jumble of toothpicks bunched together, and then the grassy prairie of Kendrick Park sprang into view.

The flattened top of Kendrick Mountain rose to the west, behind the pines edging the meadow. Kendrick is a lesser volcanic remnant that's a little older than the Peaks. We pulled over at the nearby trading post and looked back toward the San Francisco Peaks, spotting low-lying Hochderffer Hill to the east. With binoculars, we saw where a 1996 forest fire burned, in some places charring only the tops of the trees, in others burning all the way to the ground. Farther up the highway, another 1996 forest fire had burned patches on both sides of the road. The dense trees were now charcoal silhouettes, although here and there a few individuals survived.

(RIGHT) *Golden aspens nearly conceal a rustic stone cabin below the San Francisco Peaks.* ROBERT G. McDONALD

But forest fires have been through here before, as we saw later around Milepost 243. The grassy fields that had once been forest were littered with fallen logs and blackened snags. This was an old burn, one that was recovering as part of the natural cycle. I reminded myself that the aspens I had enjoyed earlier were probably a later stage of another even older burn. Aspens usually grow in land disturbed by fire, reforesting the land before the ponderosas follow.

The landscape started to change as we drove on. The road was now dropping rather than climbing, and we were seeing more piñon pine, juniper, and sagebrush. To the left, not far from the road, we saw a low, sloping mountain with a rocky red gouge in its side, almost like a quarry. This was Red Mountain, another volcanic reminder. Instead of enticing grassy meadows, the countryside was getting rockier, but there were always spots of color from the wildflowers.

Unlike tender and tasty aspen branches, scrub juniper is not favored fare for grazing animals like elk and antelope, but its dense growth offers great hiding places in this wide open country. We kept our eyes peeled in hopes of being first to spot some wildlife, but all we saw were more flowers.

At Valle Junction, U.S. Route 180 intersects with State Route 64. "Valle" is pronounced "valley," even though it's not spelled that way. Here you can head south down State 64 if you want to visit the town of Williams. We decided to turn right, going north on U.S. 180/State

Route 64 to the South Rim of the Grand Canyon. The highway goes through the town of Tusayan just before reaching the national park's entrance. Once inside the park, Route 64 turns east to Cameron and U.S. Route 89.

After Valle Junction, we were driving through what is mostly rolling rangelands with far-reaching horizons. Along the way I noticed a colorful highway marker noting that this road is also the Bushmasters Memorial Highway. State Route 64 was named the BMH to honor the Arizona and New Mexico National Guard members who fought in WWII.

The scrub and rangeland gradually gave way to tall pines along the road. The small town of Tusayan, home of the Grand Canyon Airport, lies outside the entrance to the Grand Canyon National Park. Brightly painted charter helicopters kept buzzing past the tops of the trees. We followed State Route 64 into the park. Once past the fee station, rather than heading straight to Grand Canyon Village, we turned east toward Desert View.

The highway runs through pine forest along the South Rim, with roads on the left branching off to take you toward Grand Canyon view points. Sometimes even from the highway we could see tantalizing glimpses of the Canyon's towering cliffs. Deer are a fairly common sight, so again we strained to catch a glimpse through the pines and brush. Were those antlers ... or just more branches?

Farther east on State 64 we pulled off the highway to stop at the Tusayan Ruins. Besides a museum, among

(LEFT) *Thick, stubby formations formed by molten rock reaching the surface characterize the volcanic cone inside Red Mountain in the San Francisco volcanic field.*
(OPPOSITE PAGE) *This watchtower at Desert View on the South Rim of the Grand Canyon resembles an ancient pueblo-style house. From here, you can view the Vermilion Cliffs, San Francisco Peaks, Painted Desert, and the Colorado River on the Canyon's floor.*
BOTH BY
PETER ENSENBERGER

## When You Go

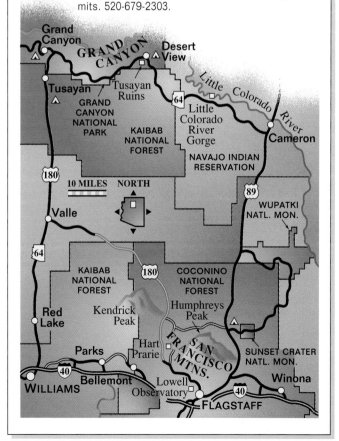

**Flagstaff Chamber of Commerce & Visitors Center:** 520-774-9541 or 800-842-7293.

**Pioneer Historical Museum:** Northern outskirts of Flagstaff on Fort Valley Road/U.S. Route 180. 520-774-6272.

**Museum of Northern Arizona:** Also on Fort Valley Road, a little beyond the historical museum. Flagstaff. 520-774-5211.

**Coconino National Forest, Flagstaff office:** Information on camping, hiking, and road conditions in the Forest. 520-527-3600. For maps and trail information on Mount Elden, Humphreys Peak, and O'Leary Peak areas, call the Peaks Ranger Station, 520-526-0866. www.fs.fed.us/r3/coconino/

**Kaibab National Forest, Tusayan Ranger Station:** Located on U.S. 180/State 64, just south of the entrance to the Grand Canyon National Park. Maps, hiking, and cross-country skiing information. 520-638-2443. www.fs.fed.us/r3/kai/

**Grand Canyon Chamber of Commerce:** 520-638-2901. www.grandcanyonchamber.org

**Grand Canyon Visitors Center:** Located three miles in from the South Entrance Station of Grand Canyon. Maps, exhibits, other Canyon information, including hikes and tours. 520-638-7888 and 638-7805 TDD. www.thecanyon.com/nps

**Cameron Trading Post:** Built in 1916 beside the Little Colorado River, it is on U.S. 89 before the bridge and just north of the junction with State Route 64 in Cameron. Motel, restaurant, stores, post office, service station. 520-679-2231 or 800-338-7385.

**Cameron Visitors Center:** The octagon building just south of the State 64/U.S. 89 junction. It has information about the Navajo Nation and sells reservation hiking and camping permits. 520-679-2303.

pine trees and junipers are the limestone block ruins of an Anasazi village. You can take the self-guided trail around the shallow storage rooms, living quarters, and kivas. One sign by a break in the trees pointed toward the San Francisco Peaks, some 48 miles or so in the distance. Although just a blue silhouette — flat, featureless, and paper-thin — the old volcano was still the dominating landmark on the horizon of the high plain.

Next, I really wanted to stop at the Desert View Watchtower, a rest stop and gift shop designed by architect Mary Colter back in 1930. Although it wasn't a replica of any single structure, Colter studied native architecture and designed the tower to look like an ancient house. The skeleton is steel on a concrete bed, but the rock faces are weathered and fitted together in the pueblo style. To go upstairs, I fed quarters into the automated turnstile. From the gift shop's window my view of the Grand Canyon and Colorado River stretched seemingly to the edge of the world. The river is about four miles away, but I could see the white rapids in the blue-green strip of water.

Desert View Watchtower is the last major viewpoint within the national park, but we had been told that State Route 64 still had more wonders in store. We weren't disappointed. Little Colorado River Gorge has two scenic overlooks that have their own breathtaking beauty. This is wild country, even though civilization is not that far away in the town of Cameron. We came out on U.S. Route 89 and turned south toward Flagstaff. ◹

# Kayenta-Monument Valley Scenic Road

*ROCK FORMATIONS AND RIPPLED SAND*

Monument Valley's monoliths rank among the most famous of the natural landmarks for film and photography buffs, an instantly recognizable skyline perhaps playing second fiddle only to the Grand Canyon. So as Chuck and I departed for Arizona's northeast corner one morning, we felt sure we were the only two people who had never seen the rock monuments firsthand.

We set out from Flagstaff, having spent the night there in order to get a jump start on the drive. We drove north on U.S. Route 89. While it had been quite cool in Flagstaff, we knew we could expect warmer weather on the Navajo Indian Reservation. Monument Valley and nearby points of interest like Page and Vermilion Cliffs are farther north than cool Flagstaff, but they are at much lower elevations so they are warmer than the Flagstaff area.

We had been driving on reservation land since passing the community of Gray Mountain, but it was after Cameron that we really began to see that we were in new territory. Strangely rounded dunes and shriveled hillocks, barren except for surreal bands of earthy pinks, blues, and greens, dotted the landscape, their crusty sides ridged and seamed with dry stream beds. I really didn't think these odd-looking mounds with the strange colors could possibly be natural, but we were seeing the northwestern edge of the Painted Desert, a badlands of bentonite clay formed from decomposing volcanic ash. The colors come from mineral deposits.

Sixteen miles north of Cameron we turned onto U.S. Route 160. Amateur paleontologists will delight in seeing the signs for dinosaur tracks; a side road leads north to where you can see these fossilized footprints.

Horses, cattle, and sheep grazed near the highway, and the scattered settlements were dotted with rounded hogans. A hogan is the traditional Navajo dwelling, usually with six or eight sides and a single east-facing door.

We stopped for fry bread in Tuba City, and I noticed my watch was an hour behind the cafe's clock. The Navajo Reservation observes daylight saving time, but the rest of Arizona does not. We also passed the turnoff for the Hopi mesas, which rise like islands surrounded by the Navajo Reservation. With more than 25,000 square miles of reservation land in Arizona, Utah, and New Mexico, the Navajo Nation is larger than West Virginia.

As we drove, we had long views of high dry plains cut by rocky gorges and exposed ridges of basalt. After passing through Tonalea, Black Mesa shouldered up on our right, with Klethla Valley spread out to the left. At one point I saw

**Name:** Kayenta-Monument Valley Scenic Road.

**Route:** From Flagstaff, U.S. Route 89 north through Cameron to U.S. Route 160; then east on 160 to Kayenta; then north on U.S. 163 to Monument Valley. The drive between Kayenta and the valley is the Monument Valley Scenic Road.

**Mileage:** 196 miles.

**Time to allow:** Two days.

**Elevation:** 6,900 feet at Flagstaff; 6,300 feet at Gray Mountain; 4,200 feet at Cameron; 5,800 feet at Kayenta.

**Overview:** From Flagstaff this is a two-day round-trip taking you deep into the Navajo Reservation. Monument Valley — a flat land with rock monoliths jutting from the valley floor — is an icon of the Southwest. Along the way you can visit volcanic cones and Indian ruins.

(OPPOSITE PAGE) *Rock formations like Yei Bichei (center) and Totem Pole (right) dramatically contrast with the sand dunes around them.* EDWARD McCAIN
(TOP) *These buttes, including the Stagecoach (center), rise in the northern part of Monument Valley.* LeROY DeJOLIE
(ABOVE) *The tones and texture of a hogan blend with the Three Sisters rock formation.* ROBERT G. McDONALD

a large metal pipe elevated on stilts above the road, running like an aqueduct from the mesa to the railroad on our left. This is a slurry pipeline that carries crushed coal that will go to the power plants in Page and in Nevada.

Near Black Mesa, Indian Route 564 leads to Navajo National Monument, site of three spectacular prehistoric Indian ruins. The Anasazi cliff dwellings of Betatakin, Keet Seel, and Inscription House (closed to visitors) date back to between A.D. 1275 and 1300. After a short hike from the visitors center to the viewpoint, you can see Betatakin from above, but to actually reach the ruins takes time and physical stamina.

The small town of Kayenta is at the junction of U.S. routes 160 and 163, the starting point of the Kayenta-Monument Valley Scenic Road. When we reached Kayenta, we impatiently checked into our motel and left directly for the rock wonders we had come so far to see.

North of Kayenta on 163 we saw the tall figures of Owl Rock on the left and Agathla Peak (sometimes called El Capitan) on the right. These rock formations are two of several volcanic necks dotting the valley.

As we neared the turnoff for Monument Valley Navajo Tribal Park, we crossed the Utah state line to reach the park entrance, but the road looped back into Arizona. At the highway fork for the park, the left turn takes you to Goulding's Trading Post, with its lodge and restaurant, nestled below a large mud-red cliff.

There's a small fee to enter Monument Valley Navajo Tribal Park. Inside the park we enjoyed the exhibits in the Information Center before driving the self-guided tour through the valley.

Out in the parking lot you can find a variety of guides and tours available if you want to leave the driving to someone else. If you drive the dirt road through Monument Valley, be aware that the speed limit is 5 mph. Think that speed is too slow? Well, we did get up to 15 mph in some sections, but for most of the drive I'd say 5 mph is just about right. Although maintained, the road is really just a wide trail at the mercies of flooding washes

(ABOVE) *As you crest a hill northeast of Kayenta, the magnificent volcanic neck named Agathla, or El Capitan, juts from the valley floor.* JERRY JACKA
(BELOW) *Owl Rock, also a volcanic neck, owes its name to natural markings.* TOM DANIELSEN
(OPPOSITE PAGE) *Monument Valley draws much of its character from the light cast on formations.* STEVE BRUNO

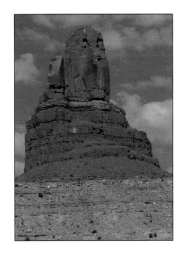

and drifting sand. A sedan can manage it, but you will want to drive slowly.

The road sloped down to the valley floor of rippled red sand. Magnificent geologic sculptures in deep, rocky reds stood against a rich blue sky. It was fun trying to figure out which formation matched which imaginative name.

Hollywood first came out here when Harry Goulding of Goulding's

Trading Post convinced movie director John Ford to visit. Since Ford filmed *Stagecoach* with John Wayne in 1938, many classic Westerns and other movie hits have been shot in Monument Valley.

Before movie crews came, before the Gouldings started trading with the Navajo, even before the Navajo named this land, Monument Valley was already ancient. The red rocks now dwarfing us had started as sediment settling in a prehistoric lowland basin. Pressure cemented the sediment into layers of sandstone and limestone. More pressure from within the earth lifted the basin floor, slowly and gradually, until there was a plateau one to three miles above sea level. Compared to that original plateau, the spires and buttes are now mere stumps, eroded down to 400 to 1,000 feet. They have been chiseled by eons of wind and water, heat and frost, sometimes the softer rock just peeling and flaking away. ◪

# When You Go

**Flagstaff-area national monuments:** About 15 miles north of Flagstaff on U.S. Route 89, Sunset Crater Volcano National Monument (520-526-0502), *www.nps.gov/sucr/,* and Wupatki National Monument (520-679-2365), *www.nps.gov/wupa/.*

**Cameron Trading Post:** Beside the Little Colorado River, on U.S. 89 before the bridge and just north of the junction with State Route 64. 520-679-2231 or 800-338-7385. Services available in Cameron include lodging, food, stores, post office, and gasoline.

**Cameron Visitors Center:** Octagonal building just south of State 64/U.S. 89 junction. Has information about the Navajo Nation and sells reservation hiking and camping permits. 520-679-2303.

**Note:** Arizona state agencies do not have jurisdiction in the Navajo Nation; government services, necessary permits, and traffic enforcement are administered by the Navajo government. Alcoholic beverages are prohibited on Navajo land by federal law.

**Navajo Nation Tourism Department:** Before your trip, call 520-871-6436 for visitors information and literature.

**Navajo Parks and Recreation Department:** Hiking and camping information and tribal permits for activities in the Navajo Nation. 520-871-6647.

**Navajo National Monument:** Turn off U.S. 160 onto State Route 564 at Black Mesa Junction and drive about nine miles to a visitors center. Betatakin (Navajo for "ledge house") can be seen from a viewpoint near the visitors center after a one-mile hike. Keet Seel (Navajo for "broken pottery") is a 16-mile hike or horse ride. Allow two days for the trek. 520-672-2366/2367. *www.nps.gov/nava*

**Monument Valley Navajo Tribal Park:** Fee. Visitors center with museum and 17-mile, self-guided scenic drive. Mitten View Campground with showers, RV hookups; fee. 435-727-3353/3287.

**Lodging and food:**

Anasazi Inn, on U.S. 160, nine miles before Kayenta. 520-697-3793.

Wetherill Inn, off U.S. 163, Kayenta. 520-697-3231.

Holiday Inn, at corner of U.S. routes 160 and 163, Kayenta. 520-697-3221 or 800-HOLIDAY.

Goulding's Lodge & Trading Post, in Utah two miles west of Monument Valley turnoff on U.S. 163. Open all year. Gift shop, lodge, museum, campground, tours. 435-727-3231.

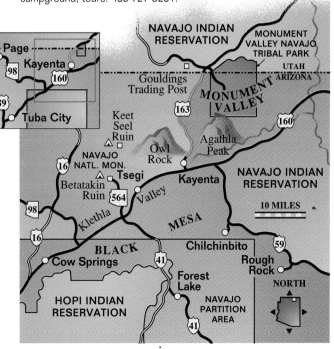

# Navajo Route 12

**Photographs by Jerry Jacka**

The scenic road that begins at Exit 357 off Interstate 40 at Lupton and ends at Canyon de Chelly obliges sightseers wanting an easy drive through a very unusual landscape. Those who haven't traveled on the Navajo Reservation in Arizona's northeast corner will be astonished by the brilliant colored rock formations, the sandstone haystacks, and towering buttes and mesas rising above tiny hogans.

The 24 miles separating Lupton from St. Michaels is like a teaser for what lies ahead. Watch the right side of the road as you leave Lupton and you'll see the graceful lion-colored cliffs of a narrow canyon running more or less parallel to the highway. After a few miles you'll see a wind-streaked sandstone cave and behind it the giant rock called the Teapot. These formations are a hint of what you'll see in the next hundred miles.

To continue on Navajo Route 12, I was supposed to take a right at its intersection with State Route 264, about 24 miles north of Lupton, but I decided to take a left to visit the historic Franciscan mission and its museum about a mile to the west. The small museum, which contains historical materials about the Franciscans' work with the Navajos, unfortunately was closed, but the building and nearby church and fields still made the stop worthwhile for photographs.

I went back to State 264 and drove east to Window Rock, the capitol of the Navajo Nation. The Navajo Reservation is the largest reservation in the United States, covering 17.6 million acres in Arizona, New Mexico, and a small part of Utah. The Navajos are also the nation's largest tribe with approximately 200,000 enrolled members. Very few of them have permanent homes at Window Rock, however, because the town is primarily a community of government offices. Many of the Navajos who live and work in Window Rock during the week vacate the place on the weekends and return to their villages on the 27,000-square-mile reservation. Gas, food, and lodging are available at Window Rock.

Before leaving Window Rock, I stopped at the flea market at the junction of State 264 and Navajo 12. I found Indians selling crafts, produce from their farms, roasted

**Name:** Navajo Route 12 from Lupton to Canyon de Chelly.

**Route:** Navajo Route 12, State Route 264, Navajo Route 64.

**Mileage:** 104 miles.

**Time to allow:** Three to four hours from Lupton.

**Elevation:** Approximately 6,000 feet at Lupton; 7,100 feet at Wheatfields Lake; 5,500 feet at Canyon de Chelly Visitors Center.

**Overview:** This route takes visitors into the heart of the Navajo Indian Reservation, a land of dramatic sandstone mesas and buttes interspersed with small communities and farmland. It ends at the rim of Canyon de Chelly, an unforgettable place of graceful sandstone cliffs where numerous petroglyphs and ancient cliff dwellings are visible.

corn, and other foods. Many Navajos were having lunch at the makeshift food stands. A couple of blocks north of the junction, on Navajo 12, there was a sign on the right (east) for Window Rock Navajo Tribal Park, a place I always like to visit when I'm in the area. The Navajo capital was named for the enormous sandstone arch towering above the tribal headquarters and the park.

Back on Navajo 12, I drove north a few miles to Fort Defiance. If you forgot to get food or gas at Window Rock, you can get them at Fort Defiance, one of the larger communities on the reservation. The fort is long gone, but it remains a painful memory for what it represented. For Navajos, it will always be associated with "The Long Walk," the single most devastating event in their history. "The Long Walk" is a reference to an event in which the U.S. Army forced some 8,000 Navajos off their homeland and marched them to Fort Sumner on the Pecos River in New Mexico, a distance of some 300 miles. They were held as prisoners there from 1864 to 1868, when a treaty established today's reservation.

At Fort Defiance, Navajo 12 turns east and crosses into New Mexico. The bright turquoise buildings of the high school on your right make a striking contrast to the orange sandstone boulders and buttes behind them. The New Mexico portion of the highway continues parallel

(OPPOSITE PAGE) *A vista on the rim of Canyon de Chelly overlooks canyons, cliffs, and farmland.*
(ABOVE) *The elements carved numerous finger-like spires from sandstone along Navajo Route 12.*

to the Arizona border for about 40 miles, gradually rising through the sparsely populated landscape to an altitude of 7,100 feet before crossing back into Arizona at Wheatfields Lake, where I took a coffee break and enjoyed the fragrance of the ponderosa pine trees around me.

I was not eager to leave, but I knew the scenery on the second half of this drive would be exceptional, and I also wanted to leave time for a stop at Navajo Community College in Tsaile, about 40 miles northwest of Wheatfields. The road to Tsaile passes through wide valleys covered with sage and small juniper and pine trees, and offers great views of the Chuska and Lukachukai Mountains, contiguous ranges sometimes referred to as the Navajo Alps.

Navajo Community College is hard to miss because its main building, the four-story Hatahli Center, is the tallest man-made structure for many miles around, and it is shaped like a stylized hogan (the six- or eight-sided structures that dot the reservation). An excellent museum occupies the second and third floors of the building. In addition to fine examples of Navajo crafts, the exhibits include dozens of historic photographs and rare artifacts of the Anasazi Indians, who inhabited the Four Corners region before the Navajos arrived. The college press is also in the building, on the first floor, and it's a good place to find books about the Navajos you may not see elsewhere.

It is only 24 miles from Tsaile to Canyon de Chelly and Chinle, but you can see the canyon at three viewpoints long before you get to Chinle. Chinle, however, is the only convenient place to stay overnight in the area. There are three motels, gas stations, and several places to eat.

When I left Tsaile, the time of day photographers

(ABOVE, LEFT) *Wind and erosion sculpted Window Rock from Kayenta sandstone. The Navajo tribal capital drew its name from the formation.*
(LEFT) *Sage and juniper vegetate a wide valley spreading from the Chuska Mountains near Lukachukai. Remains of an ancient lava flow cap some sandstone cliffs in the range.*
(OPPOSITE PAGE)
*The traditional hogan inspired the design of the four-story Hatahli Center at Navajo Community College in Tsaile. A museum occupies two floors of the building.*

call "the magic hour" was rapidly approaching. The "magic" occurs when the sun has nearly set and the light softens to burnt ochre on the surrounding cliffs and mesas and long shadows lie down in the canyons. The road from Tsaile to Chinle is also referred to as the North Rim Drive because it runs parallel to the canyon. Canyon de Chelly looks like a V lying on its side, with the narrow end at Chinle. It is actually two canyons — Canyon del Muerto, visible from the North Rim, and Canyon de Chelly, visible from the South Rim. I had spent time in both canyons and I would be hard-pressed to tell one from the other without a compass.

Both canyons are like a snippet of the Grand Canyon. Dramatic sandstone cliffs, many streaked in black or white where various minerals have leached through the porous stone, line the canyons and rise between 300 and 1,000 feet. Both Grand Canyon and Canyon de Chelly are national parks, but one of the major differences between them is that Navajo families still use Canyon de Chelly. From either rim you can see a hogan or cabin, cultivated fields, and orchards spreading on the banks of creeks, and usually a Navajo tending sheep nearby.

There is no "best" way to see this canyon. I've visited all of the overlooks, taken a jeep tour through the bottom, and hiked the 3-mile round-trip trail from the South Rim to White House Ruin. On this trip I had a friend along who had never seen Canyon de Chelly before. Standing at an overlook on the North Rim in the late afternoon, he commented, "In my entire life I have never seen anything as beautiful as this." That sentiment holds true, I think, no matter where you are when you see Canyon de Chelly.

# When You Go

**Note:** Arizona state agencies have no jurisdiction in the Navajo Nation; government services, permits, and traffic enforcement are administered by the Navajo government. Alcoholic beverages prohibited on Navajo land by federal law.

**Navajo Nation Tourism Department:** Window Rock. 520-871-6436.

**Lodging:** Navajo Nation Inn, Window Rock. 800-662-6189.

Rainbow Inn, Tsaile. 520-724-6830.

Best Western Canyon de Chelly, Chinle. 800-327-0354.

Holiday Inn, Chinle. 800-HOLIDAY.

Thunderbird Lodge, Chinle. 800-679-2473.

**Canyon de Chelly National Monument:** Group tours conducted on six-wheel-drive vehicles at the canyon's bottom year-round (Thunderbird Lodge, reservations: 800-679-2473), but winters are very cold, summers very hot. Individual tours also available on horseback or four-wheel-drive vehicle; Canyon de Chelly Visitors Center, 520-674-5500. www.nps.gov/cach/

**Camping:** Wheatfields Lake, 44 miles northeast of Window Rock on Navajo Route 12 at 7,100 feet altitude; fishing; picnic tables, fire pits, outhouses. No drinking water. Summer, fall only.

Cottonwood Campground, a half mile from the Canyon de Chelly Visitors Center. Restrooms, picnic tables, water, dump station. No-fee area. 520-674-5500.

Spider Rock RV and Camping, a Navajo-owned campground 10 miles east of the visitors center on the South Rim Drive; tent sites, no hookups for RVs; solar showers, open fire pits. 520-674-8261.

**Services:** Food and gas may be purchased at Window Rock, Fort Defiance, Tsaile, and Chinle.

*(This chapter was researched and written by Sam Negri.)*

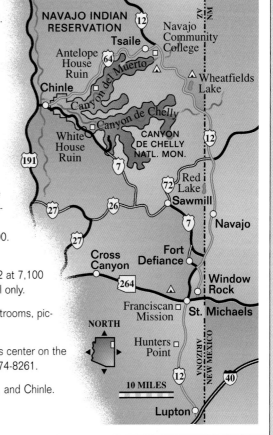

# Fredonia-Vermilion Cliffs Scenic Road

**Photographs by Randy A. Prentice**

Nothing rewards the weary motorist better than the Arizona Strip. And weary motorist you may be, after you dare to venture all the way to the top of the state. Trust me, the drive between Bitter Springs and Fredonia is worth every crick in your neck. Plus, there are some exciting things to do on both ends of the stretch.

Our family began the trip in Page, the closest town to the small Navajo community of Bitter Springs. Page, of course, is on the shores of Lake Powell, which laps at the sandstone walls forming Glen Canyon.

We spent our first day in a rental boat, skimming about Lake Powell's warm, blue waters and touring through Antelope Canyon. Visiting Glen Canyon Dam afforded much excitement. Watch out for those monsoons, though, if you happen to be on the lake in the summer.

The next day, we journeyed through the pass on U.S. Route 89 toward Bitter Springs to begin our scenic road trip. Echo Peaks jut majestically toward the sky on the right, while Red Mesa rises out of Echo Cliffs on the left. We could see Marble Canyon, a narrow crack between the 1,800-foot-high Echo Cliffs and the 3,000-foot-high Vermilion Cliffs; House Rock Valley stretching wide toward the horizon; and the Grand Canyon just beginning to crack open the earth.

Navajo Bridge crosses the Colorado River downstream from historic Lees Ferry, approximately 14 miles up U.S. 89A from Bitter Springs. Stop and walk along the old

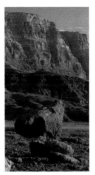

**Name:** Fredonia to Vermilion Cliffs Scenic Road.

**Route:** From Page, go southwest on U.S. Route 89 to Bitter Springs, the start of the scenic route. From there, go northwest on U.S. Alternate Route 89 (89A).

**Mileage:** 104 miles, Page to Fredonia.

**Time to allow:** All day.

**Elevation:** 4,400 feet at Page; 7,900 feet at Jacob Lake; 3,500 feet at Fredonia.

**Overview:** Two of Arizona's scenic roads wind through the Kaibab Plateau's remote Arizona Strip north of the Grand Canyon. This one goes by Jacob Lake and continues to the back side of the Kaibab Plateau and fantastic views of mountains, valleys, and cliffs.

bridge as cars pass on the new one. We inspected a bolt used to bind the new bridge during construction — it was bigger than Michael!

Down below, the Colorado River flows through Marble Canyon, which is 467 feet deep and 600 feet wide at the bridge. Just upstream, Marble Canyon marks the official beginning of the Grand Canyon.

To the southwest, Marble Canyon Lodge, Lees Ferry Lodge, and Cliff Dwellers Lodge offer lodging, plus food and good conversation. After another mile or two, we pulled over to explore rock formations lining the north side of the road at the base of the Vermilion Cliffs. A house is built in one; another looks like a giant ice cream cone.

House Rock Valley stretches endlessly to the south and southwest. As the winding highway begins to climb the Kaibab Plateau, the landscape changes from desert scrub to terrain dominated by piñon and juniper trees.

The Kaibab Plateau towers 3,000 feet above House Rock Valley. Stopping at the lookout point we could see the valley, plus Echo Cliffs and the Vermilion Cliffs in the distance. The Vermilion Cliffs are always red — the particular shade depends on the time of day. I love to see them in the late afternoon sun, when mere red becomes glowing magenta streaked with shadowed plum.

As you continue up into the plateau, you will see the junipers and piñons give way to conifer forests, dominated by ponderosa pines. Look, too, for white fir,

(OPPOSITE PAGE) *At Navajo Bridge, the Colorado River flows lazily before rushing through the Grand Canyon.*
(ABOVE, RIGHT) *The Vermilion Cliffs form a part of the eastern boundary of the Arizona Strip.*
(ABOVE) *Wahweap Marina occupies a niche just above Glen Canyon Dam.*

Douglas fir, Gambel oaks, and lovely quaking aspens.

Jacob Lake appears as a bustling corner of 89A and U.S. 64 — the latter is the Kaibab Plateau-North Rim Parkway discussed in the following chapter. Stop here for refreshments since it's the last town before Fredonia, roughly 40 miles away.

As we drove out of the Jacob Lake area, it began to sprinkle lightly, and the pungent smell of pine needles and mountain rain filled the air. Several times we ventured off the paved road onto dirt roads in our four-wheel-drive vehicle to explore the wooded areas beyond the roadway.

Le Fevre Scenic Overlook rests about halfway between Jacob Lake and Fredonia, just before descending the backside of the Kaibab Plateau. Since we had caught glimpses of the amazing views between the trees, we decided to stop for a better look.

And what a look! The broad Johnson Wash (some locals call it Johnson Run) extends toward the red-shale Shinarump Cliffs resting on the far horizon beyond Fredonia. Behind the cliffs we could see sandstone promontories stretching into Utah.

Our last 20 miles took us down the plateau, through piñons and junipers again, before entering the grassy plain of Johnson Run and Fredonia, the official end of the scenic road. We easily found our motel, the Crazy Jug, and the owner gave us the rundown on where to eat, get gas, and that sort of thing, and directions to Pipe Spring National Monument and Toroweap.

Pipe Spring is 14 miles west of Fredonia on State Route 389. Ranching began there in 1858, and Mormon leader Brigham Young decided to locate church herds there after a treaty was signed with the Navajos in 1870. Arizona's first telegraph opened there in 1871.

Six miles east of Pipe Spring we turned off of 389 onto a dirt road at a sign that read "Mount Trumbull." It's 61 miles over dirt roads that can be anywhere from well-graded to pretty hairy, so don't try this without a high-clearance vehicle. You won't need a four-wheel drive, however. And don't start out with anything less than a FULL tank of gas!

We began with a half-tank, thinking we would be safe since we'd made it all the way from Phoenix to Page on just half a tank. But as we pulled up at the canyon's edge (literally) we were down to an eighth of a tank or less. So running out of gas plagued my thoughts as I crept toward the canyon with Kelsey. Chuck and Michael had chosen another spot about 20 feet away.

As we approached, a feeling of dread came over me. Me, who loves the scariest rides and is not afraid of heights. About 10 feet from the edge I dropped to my knees. At five feet I was crawling on my belly like a snake, clutching Kelsey's dress in my fist. By the time we got to the edge, my stomach was lodged in my throat.

But what a magnificent sight! We stared breathlessly into an enormous chasm, 3,000 feet straight down. Even from such heights, the Colorado River is so wide it looks as though it's right there. Toroweap offers stunning views and tricky optical illusions not found on either the North or South Rim of the Grand Canyon. Although we lay still at the edge, I felt some unknown force was trying mightily to suck us off our precarious perch. Looking over, I saw the guys on their bellies too, so I didn't feel like such a sissy. A great roar sounded in our ears, and eventually we climbed back away from the edge and began to pick our way along the rim about 150 feet, until we caught sight of Lava Falls below in the river.

Be careful as you leave — signs often point in the wrong direction. The way out is the way you came in.

I sent up a stream of prayers, asking that we please not run out of gas, and thank heaven we didn't. As we gassed up in Fredonia, preparing to head back to Phoenix, we all breathed a sigh of contentment, and relief. ✂

(OPPOSITE PAGE, TOP) *Sprawling on both sides of 89A, House Rock Valley reaches north and east to the Vermilion Cliffs and south nearly to the Grand Canyon.* (OPPOSITE PAGE, BOTTOM) *Picturesque Pipe Spring National Monument preserves a fortified Mormon ranch established in the 1870s.* W. D. WRAY (RIGHT) *Toroweap Point towers more than 3,000 feet over the Colorado River.*

# When You Go

**Page-Lake Powell Chamber of Commerce:** Information on local sights and services, tour bookings for lake and river tours, scenic flights. 520-645-2741.

**Lake Powell Resorts and Marinas, Page:** Marina services, boat rentals, boat tours, lodging, RV parks. Reservations, 800-528-6154, or 602-278-8888 in the greater Phoenix area.

**Note:** Arizona state agencies do not have jurisdiction in the Navajo Nation; government services, necessary permits, and traffic enforcement are administered by the Navajo government. Alcoholic beverages are prohibited on Navajo land by federal law.

**Navajo Nation Tourism Department:** Provides visitor information and literature. 520-871-6436.

**Navajo Parks and Recreation Department:** Hiking and camping information, as well as tribal permits for activities on the Navajo Nation. 520-871-6647.

**Fredonia Chamber of Commerce:** 520-643-7241.

**Kaibab National Forest, North Kaibab Ranger District:** Maps, hiking, backroads information. Fredonia. 520-643-7395. Kaibab Plateau Visitor Center, Jacob Lake. 520-643-7298.

**Pipe Spring National Monument:** 520-643-7105. *www.nps.gov/pisp/*

**Lodging and food:**

Marble Canyon Lodge, U.S. 89A at Lees Ferry turnoff. Store, restaurant, post office, self-serve laundry, coin showers, gas station. 520-355-2225 or 800-726-1789.

Lees Ferry Lodge, three miles west of Marble Canyon on U.S. 89A. Dramatic views of Vermilion Cliffs, Echo Cliffs, Marble Canyon. Restaurant, gift shop, sporting goods. 520-355-2230/2231.

Cliff Dweller's Lodge, eight miles west of Marble Canyon on U.S 89A. Motel rooms, restaurant, small store, gas station. 520-355-2228.

Jacob Lake Inn, 45 miles north of the North Rim on U.S. 89A. Open all year. Rooms, cabins, gift shop, groceries, gas station. 520-643-7232.

Kaibab Camper Village, tent spaces and RV sites. 520-643-7804.

# Kaibab Plateau-North Rim Parkway

*THE GRANDER SIDE OF THE GRAND CANYON*

**Photographs by Randy A. Prentice**

**Name:** Kaibab Plateau-North Rim Scenic Parkway.

**Route:** From Page, take U.S. Route 89 to Bitter Springs and then U.S. Alternate Route 89 (89A) to Jacob Lake. Then, go to the North Rim on State Route 67 — designated a scenic parkway between Jacob Lake and the North Rim. From Flagstaff, go north on U.S. 89 to 89A at Bitter Springs.

**Mileage:** 125 miles from Page; 211 miles from Flagstaff.

**Time to allow:** All day.

**Elevation:** 4,400 feet at Page; 7,900 feet at Jacob Lake; 8,200 feet at the North Rim.

**Overview:** This is the second of two drives into the Arizona Strip. They meet at Jacob Lake. This trip takes you through the heart of the Kaibab Plateau to the remote North Rim of the Grand Canyon.

The Grand Canyon. At 277 miles long, up to 18 miles across, and one mile deep, it boggles the minds of nearly five million visitors every year. Yet with all that great expanse, so many people only see the views from the South Rim. Our drive would take us to the North Rim — higher up, more isolated, and, from all accounts, definitely worth the longer drive.

The journey to the North Rim crosses some of Arizona's most colorfully diverse territory, and we had seen some of it on our way to Fredonia (see previous chapter). Although we had started from Page, you can start your trip heading north from Flagstaff on U.S. Route 89. Take U.S. 89 until you reach the reservation town of Bitter Springs. From there, take U.S. 89A to Jacob Lake. Coming from Page, this is where we turned onto U.S. 89A, too.

The Kaibab Plateau-North Rim Parkway begins near Jacob Lake, a small hamlet named for 19th-century Mormon settler Jacob Hamblin. Major John Wesley Powell, famous Grand Canyon explorer, also used this route to cross the Kaibab Plateau in the early 1870s. At the junction of State 67 and U.S. 89A, stop at the Forest Service visitors center for maps, books, and other information about the drive.

Huge ponderosa pines grow in thick stands along the highway, which was under construction when we went

through. This is a modern paved highway, but our lane was down to the dirt at that point. While bumpy, it seemed fitting in this back-country setting to give us an inkling of what travel through here might have been like so long ago. The kids spotted several deer in the forest.

Twelve miles south of the visitors center, a Forest Service road leads adventure-seekers to the Jacob Lake Lookout Tower. It's six miles on a decent road, fit for most high-clearance vehicles. The tower offers super views of the surrounding countryside. It's worth a look if you have time.

Eventually, rolling meadows break apart the thickly clustered pines, filling the roadsides with tall, wispy yellow-green prairie grasses. Yellow and blue wildflowers grow profusely amidst the grasses, and mule deer sometimes browse in the meadows, mindless of passing vehicles. Other wildlife, such as elk, black bear, weasels, skunks, and badgers, also make their homes in the area.

About five miles before reaching Grand Canyon National Park, we made a quick pit stop at the one little roadside market between Jacob Lake and the North Rim. Here we noticed heavy hints for water conservation. With the green trees and grasses all around, I was surprised to learn that the Kaibab Plateau has very little water. There are only

(OPPOSITE PAGE) *Maple trees dressed for fall decorate a North Rim hillside overlooking two conical formations — Brahma and Deva — called temples. Nearly 100 miles away, the San Francisco Peaks rise on the horizon.*

(ABOVE, RIGHT) *Scenic State Route 67 cuts through a dense pine forest between Jacob Lake and the North Rim.*

(ABOVE) *A mule deer forages at dusk near Point Imperial.*

a few small springs, and rainfall and snowmelt drains through the plateau's porous limestone, sometimes seeping through the walls of the Grand Canyon. Because the North Rim has no natural source for drinking water, the national park pumps its water up from Roaring Springs.

Nearing the summit of the plateau, blue and Englemann spruce line the meadows, along with white and Douglas fir and a lavish smattering of Rocky Mountain quaking aspen, which give a red-gold splash of color in the fall. These are the trees that appear to "shimmer."

After paying to get into Grand Canyon National Park, we drove a few more miles to the Grand Canyon Lodge at Bright Angel Point. To the east of the lodge is Bright Angel Canyon, to the west is Transept Canyon, both easily seen from viewpoints. We parked the car and walked a short distance on one of the nearby trails. Coming out of the forest's piney shade, we found ourselves teetering on the brink of the Canyon's sun-shot panorama. Our mountain drive had taken us to the top of the world.

Even the Grand Canyon Lodge itself, hanging on the

very lip of the Canyon at Bright Angel Point, is a small piece of architectural scenery. Rebuilt in 1937 (the first one burned down) of local stone and ponderosa timbers, the lodge has a lobby the size of a small church with huge windows looking out over the Canyon in three directions. For an open-air view of the Canyon, you can sit on the

## When You Go

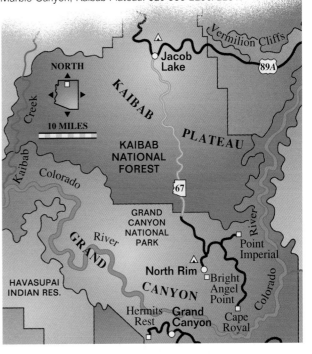

terrace with the outdoor fireplace behind you. Well, it looks like a fireplace, but you could park a Yugo in it.

Several self-guided hiking trails offer spectacular views of the Canyon if you want to wander unfettered by tour groups, but highly informative guided tours are also available.

Lodging at the top of the North Rim is limited, and even campgrounds require reservations. Besides the Grand Canyon Lodge, Kaibab Lodge is visible from the highway about five miles before you reach the park entrance. Jacob Lake Inn, at the beginning of the route, has rooms, cabins, and a campground. ◍

(OPPOSITE PAGE, ABOVE) *The Colorado River seems tiny when it is viewed through 50-foot-high Angels Window.*
(OPPOSITE PAGE, BELOW) *Builders used native wood and stone for the North Rim's Grand Canyon Lodge.*
(ABOVE) *Only a few people tred to Cape Final on the North Rim of the Grand Canyon.*

# Historic Route 66

*FROM FLAGSTAFF TO KINGMAN*

Photographs by David Elms Jr.

**Name:** Historic Route 66.

**Route:** Interstate 40 and old Route 66.

**Mileage:** 150 miles, Flagstaff to Kingman.

**Time to allow:** Five to seven hours.

**Elevation:** 6,900 feet at Flagstaff; 6,800 feet at Williams; 5,250 feet at Seligman; 3,300 feet at Kingman.

**Overview:** Designated "historic" by the Arizona Parkways, Historic and Scenic Roads program are stretches in — east to west — Holbrook, Joseph City, Winslow, Flagstaff, and Williams. Also, the route from Seligman to Kingman carries the designation. This drive, although designated for its historic value, affords grand scenery in Arizona's high country.

Leaning against a pole in Flagstaff, I gawked at the hot-pink neon signs and weathered brick storefronts lining the street. All around me the young and young at heart wandered on the sidewalks. Signs dangling from lamp posts, posted in windows, or painted on the sides of buildings hailed an era long vanished. Above my head, a large pine-colored street sign explained it all: Historic Route 66.

I stood on the doorstep of an exciting journey, not just across the miles, but through time. For a moment I imagined the trek as Lt. Edward F. (Ned) Beale found it in 1857 — roaming untamed territory, charting a route for the railroad to follow. Beale traveled across Arizona with 50 men and 22 camels purchased by the Army. Although his main purpose was to survey the road, military officials were also interested in whether the beasts could adapt to harsh climates and serve military purposes in the West. Officials apparently had not counted on the soldiers' inability to adapt to the spitting, stinking animals, however, and the "camel experiment" never was attempted again. The Beale Road, though, was followed by the railroad and Route 66, and at places all three virtually run side by side.

Not too old for make-believe, I walked to my car and imagined being in Beale's group, headed for my unwanted camel. That illusion shattered when my fingers brushed the metal door handle of the small, rented compact car. Immediately I was instead slipping into a shiny car, its engine roaring, ready for adventure. With a little imagination, the magic of Route 66 is timeless.

Nicknamed the "Main Street of America," Route 66 served as the main street of hundreds of towns along its path. It wound across scenery most Americans only saw in magazines and movies. Stretching 2,448 miles to link Chicago and Los Angeles, Route 66 led to hope and adventure. In the 1920s, drivers eked across the countryside on this road before it was fully paved. When the Great Depression gripped the nation, Route 66 carried thousands of displaced Dust Bowl refugees toward promises of new life and jobs in the West.

By 1984, the old road had finally yielded to Interstate

*(OPPOSITE PAGE) Garland Prairie Vista offers a remote view of the San Francisco Peaks as well as a picnic area for travelers along Route 66 west of Flagstaff. (ABOVE) Traffic on Route 66 in Flagstaff streams past motels and restaurants.*

40. Now a cultural icon, Route 66 conjures images of days gone by, capturing the spirit of *The Grapes of Wrath*. More than 200 of its historical miles stretch across Arizona, beckoning travelers to re-visit it if they remember it and to discover it if they don't.

East of Flagstaff, brief stretches of Route 66 serve as local roads in the towns of Holbrook, Joseph City, and Winslow, and are a part of Arizona's scenic and historic road program.

Holbrook is a stepping-off point for the Petrified Forest and the Painted Desert, via U.S. Route 180 or I-40 east of town. Also in Holbrook are the Pow Wow Trading Post, which glitters with neon at night, and the Wigwam Village motel, where you can sleep in a motel designed as a tepee.

In Joseph City, the old Jackrabbit Trading Post (520-288-3230) keeps its doors open along the old route. It sells Indian jewelry, Mexican crafts, and a variety of souvenirs.

At Winslow, take Exit 264 from I-40 and you'll be on Hibbard Road, a section of which harbors the flavor of the old road. About four miles east of town, State Route 87 takes you (one mile from the interstate) to Homolovi Ruins State Park (520-289-2021), a site where ancestors of the Hopi Indians lived 800 years ago.

In Flagstaff, the old road is Santa Fe Avenue or Business Loop 40. Historic Route 66 can be accessed from I-40 or I-17 at several points.

At one stop for gas and coffee in Flagstaff we also got advice from the store attendant. "Don't forget the Crookton

The rain held off long enough for us to marvel at the huge, old engine displayed on the tracks of the Williams-Grand Canyon Railroad. After taking several pictures, we headed next door to the visitors center, which used to be the old train depot. Inside are the original floor scale and the names of passengers scribbled on the walls. When we asked about that, we learned that freight was set along the walls, with each owner's name scribbled above it for identification. There are lots of dates on the walls too, dating to the turn of the century.

The visitors center is operated jointly by the Forest Service, the city of Williams, Williams-Grand Canyon Chamber of Commerce, and the Southwest Natural and Cultural Heritage Association. The center gives away pamphlets listing motels and restaurants and the Williams Free Hometown Map and Guide, which describes auto, bike, and hiking tours in and around Williams and the Kaibab National Forest.

We took Route 66 (sometimes in the past called Bill Williams Avenue) past the old buildings, storefronts and

Road turnoff," he said. We nodded, having read about that part of the old alignment, and assured him we wouldn't miss it. Then we were off on I-40 for the first leg of our journey.

If you don't mind some driving on gravel, exit I-40 about 10 miles west of Flagstaff at Bellemont, turn left on Transwestern Road, and mosey through Brannigan Park. You'll pass over the highest point of Route 66 anywhere — this stretch through the ponderosa pines is 7,300 feet above sea level and winds past early 1900s homesteads and businesses that closed when the road was realigned farther south in 1942. From there, you go through Parks and Pittman Valley before arriving in Williams.

For a less grueling stretch, stay on I-40 at Bellemont until you reach Parks. Here you'll head west for six stunning miles past Garland Prairie Vista. Stop here for a picnic and enjoy a spectacular view of the San Francisco Peaks. We dallied here for a while, frolicking in the cool air and warm prairie grasses.

Then we were off again on the old road. Soon the Oak Hill Snow Play Area (formerly Williams ski area) appeared, beckoning us to step out of the car again. Picnicking is good here, too, and we left a happy group enjoying their feast as we drove off for Williams.

We rejoined I-40 at Deer Farm Road. You can stay on the old alignment and pass over a part of the Old Trails Highway, but ominous clouds were approaching quickly, and we didn't want to get caught on an unpaved road in the rain. We continued on I-40 and got off at Exit 165, which took us to the center of Williams and a one-way loop drive formed by Railroad Avenue and Route 66.

(ABOVE)  *A courtyard just off Route 66
in Flagstaff attracts people to shops and restaurants.*
(BELOW) *The Grand Canyon steam train pulls
out of the Williams station on a bright, crisp morning.*
(OPPOSITE PAGE, ABOVE) *An old gas pump and signs
outside of Seligman suggest the flavor of earlier days.*
(OPPOSITE PAGE, BELOW) *Juan Delgadillo's Snow Cap
restaurant on Historic Route 66 in Seligman attracts
visitors from around the world.*

businesses along the street. We thought time must certainly stand still in Williams.

After cruising several times through town, we drove up the hill on Sixth Street to the Forest Service station and spoke with Teri Cleeland, resident historian. I would venture to guess that Teri knows as much as anyone about Route 66, and she spent an hour or so explaining the different alignments to us. And of course, she reminded us of Williams' special mention in the history books.

"We had the last stoplight between Chicago and L.A.," she boasted.

Teri also advised that while exploring can be fun along the old road, it's better to follow the auto tours or leave the car and take a mountain bike tour. "Some of that old 1930s pavement is not so hot to drive on," she told us. "The last major improvements were made to Route 66 in the 1940s and 1950s, and it was decertified in 1985. So it's been a while since anything's been done to it."

The skies were clearing now. As we left, Teri waved and reminded us not to miss the Crookton Road Exit (Exit 139). We smiled and thought of the convenience store clerk in Flagstaff.

Speeding along I-40, we veered off at the Crookton Road Exit near Ash Fork, and continued parallel to I-40 for a while before angling north. Suddenly, we were in the middle of nowhere, or so it seemed. Wonderful old roadbed beckoned us to travel at a more cautious, more gentle, pace. Wide expanses of meadowland stretched all around us, and we felt that we were experiencing what it was like for travelers in 1920s and '30s — all that countryside and not a soul around. Lonely, but so liberating at the same time. We felt free! Just as I felt a rousing rendition of *America the Beautiful* stirring inside me, we happened upon a bridge, alongside a newer one, east of Seligman.

Then everything hushed for a moment. Chuck pulled our car to the side of the road and shut off the engine. In the immense stillness, we walked quietly onto the old bridge, grasped the crumbling cement, and stared in rapt fascination across the wheat-colored fields. A small herd of horses

grazed quietly, great purple mountains looming in the distance behind them.

Running beneath the older bridge, the old Santa Fe Railroad tracks extended across those fields, into the horizon. We stood quietly for a long while before I turned and saw the train approaching from the west. Our excitement mounted as we watched it come closer and closer. When it finally sped beneath us, we leaned out from the bridge, straining to snap pictures as the train raced by to vanish into the eastern horizon. For us, the spirit of Route 66 was captured at that spot, on that old bridge, over the train tracks and in the surrounding countryside. It was difficult to leave, knowing that the crumbling old bridge must someday succumb to age. Reluctantly, we got back in our car and drove on.

Our disappointment in leaving the bridge didn't last long, for there were many more sights to see. When we arrived in Seligman after just a few minutes, we saw that old Route 66 runs along the backs of some of the buildings, because an even older alignment used to run through town and was later moved to where it rests now. It's here in Seligman that the state's historic designation begins.

We quenched our thirst at Delgadillo's Snow Cap Drive-In, then wandered next door to the barbershop to meet Angel Delgadillo.

Angel, with his brother Juan, spearheaded the effort to preserve Route 66 around Seligman and knows a lot about the road's heyday. He was there for much of it. Beneath wispy, white hair he sports a weathered brown complexion and laughing, kind eyes. He grins a lot, loves to chat, and people passing near Seligman are missing out if they don't stop in — either at the barbershop or at the adjacent Route 66 Gift Shop and Museum — to say hi and listen to him for a bit.

The Route 66 Gift Shop and Museum acts as a small visitors center and holds an extensive collection of Route 66 memorabilia. Some is for sale; other treasures are just for viewing. All of it merits inspection, and I don't know how many times we exclaimed, "Oh wow, remember that."

We left Seligman, waving good-bye to the barbershop occupants, and headed west again. The old road loops northward, and when we were almost to Peach Springs, we could see the western edges of the Grand Canyon in the distance. It's really an incredible sight.

We passed the Frontier Cafe in Truxton, known for good food and friendly locals, and then continued to Hackberry, where we poked around for a while, admiring the Black Mountains to the west, the Grand Canyon formations still visible to the north, and the vast, spreading countryside all around.

After another short sprint of about 20 miles, we found ourselves cruising past piles of black rock called Peach Springs tuff, actually fused debris from a collapsed volcanic crater. Nancy Riggs, a volcanologist I spoke with later at Northern Arizona University, said the entire area surrounding Kingman was alive with volcanic activity between 25 million and 50 million years ago.

In fact, as I spoke with Bob Yost of the Mohave Museum of History and Art in Kingman, he told me the whole town of Kingman sits in an ancient crater.

"We hope it's ancient anyway," he added wryly.

Entering Kingman, Route 66 becomes Andy Devine Avenue, named after the town's most famous resident, who was a character actor in Western movies. As you wind through town, the strip still boasts a number of

(ABOVE, LEFT) *Now semi-retired, barber Angel Delgadillo became a driving force behind efforts to preserve Historic Route 66 in the Seligman area.* (BELOW) *An authentic 1930's roadside service station in Hackberry is being preserved as a visitors center.*

original hot spots. Mr. D'z Diner is down the road a ways, next to the Dream Machine, which is a good place to stop if you want to see some of the cars that might have cruised Route 66 in its heyday.

Kingman is a good place to spend the night. The Kingman Chamber of Commerce, located in the Powerhouse Visitor Center, has put together auto tours covering some of the historic spots in town. The Historic Route 66 Association, also located in the historic Powerhouse building, has memorabilia, literature, and anecdotes about the old road.

But believe me, if you decide to get your kicks along old Route 66, you'll have a few favorite anecdotes of your own to share. 🐾

(LEFT) *A memorial in Kingman honors Lt. Edward F. Beale for his trailblazing and brave adventures.*
(BELOW) *An adventurer prepares to enter the Lava River Cave in the Coconino National Forest. Officials urge that only experienced cavers enter the cave.*

# When You Go

**Flagstaff Visitors Center:** 520-774-9541 or 800-842-7293.

**Flagstaff Convention & Visitors Bureau:** 520-779-7611.

**Grand Canyon Deer Farm:** Fee. 25 miles west of Flagstaff on Interstate 40 at Exit 171, Deer Farm Rd. 800-926-3337.

**Williams and Forest Service Visitors Center:** 800-863-0546 or 520-635-4061.

**Ash Fork Visitor Center:** 520-637-0204.

**Kingman Area Chamber of Commerce:** 520-753-6106.

**Seligman Chamber of Commerce:** 520-422-3939.

**Route 66 Gift Shop/Museum/Visitors Center:** Seligman. 520-422-3352. *www.route66giftshop.com* lists local lodging and eateries.

**Powerhouse Visitor Center:** Kingman. 520-753-6132.

**Historic Route 66 Association:** Kingman. 520-753-5001.

**Mohave Museum of History and Art:** Kingman. 520-753-3195.

**Grand Canyon Caverns:** One of the world's largest dry cave systems, 21 stories below the surface. Accessible paths, tours. About 25 miles west of Seligman. Fee. 520-422-3223.

**Lava River Cave:** From Flagstaff take I-40 nine miles west to Bellemont Exit, turn right, then left on Historic Route 66. Take first Forest Service road to the right (FR 171) for seven miles, then FR 171B to the cave. No facilities. Cavers should be experienced, bring own light, dress warmly, wear thick-soled shoes. No pets. Coconino National Forest, Peaks Ranger District, 520-526-0866.

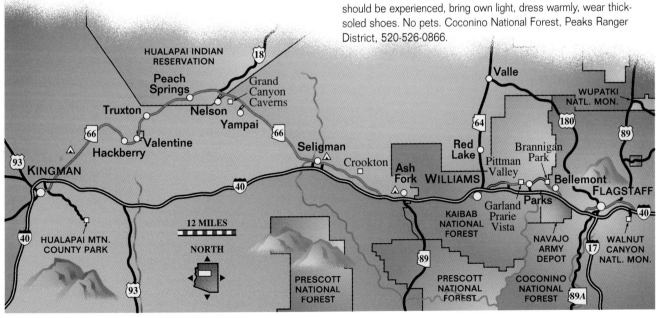

# Historic Route 66

**Photographs by David Elms Jr.**

Oatman Road, also known as the Mohave County Highway, tests your driving skills, not to mention your mettle.

Oatman Road takes you on a trek into the heart of the Black Mountains, with often-nasty hairpin switchbacks clinging to the side of the mountains at dizzying heights. Those who prefer to be a bit closer to the ground or who drive high-profile RVs might want to skip this road. But let me challenge you to find the willpower, the nerve, and the right vehicle for the trip — I guarantee it's worth the effort and a few gray hairs.

Continuing on from our previous journey, which had taken us from Flagstaff to Kingman over much of old Route 66, Chuck and I were now headed for Oatman, a gold-mining town established in 1911. Town founders named the town after the Oatman family, most of whom were killed by Indians in 1851. Before it faded in the 1930s, the Oatman area reportedly produced two million ounces of gold. In the early 1950s, the town lost Route 66, which was rerouted farther south.

From Kingman we traveled west on Route 66 for about five miles to McConnico. (Actually, you travel south out of Kingman but the interstate directional signs say west.) Turning west at the underpass below Interstate 40, we continued on the old route, now named Oatman Road. The heat was sweltering as we fled deeper into the desert,

**Name:** Historic Route 66.

**Route:** Oatman Road.

**Mileage:** 57 miles, Kingman to Golden Shores.

**Time to allow:** All day.

**Elevation:** 3,300 feet at Kingman; 3,000 feet at Oatman; 500 feet at Golden Shores.

**Overview:** You'll drive over rough, twisting roads and pass through the Sacramento Valley and the Black Mountains en route to Oatman, an old gold-mining town that hangs on as a tourist attraction with scores of burros roaming the streets. From Oatman, the route continues on to the Colorado River.

and before long we were longing for Cool Springs Camp. When we arrived, we decided the town's name is the dirtiest trick anyone can play on a hot, thirsty traveler. The place isn't cool, and there are no springs in sight. We spotted a neat Route 66 highway sign painted on the road — you know, the kind that looks good from an aerial view. So Chuck stopped the car right there in the middle of the road and climbed up onto the roof to try to take a picture. I watched the road to make sure no one plowed into us from behind. I needn't have bothered.

We drove on, slowly swallowed up by the desert, glad we had brought our own water, soda, and food. It looked like we might use all of it before civilization sprang up again. The Black Mountains loomed ominously before us and our subcompact wagon whined as we forced it up, up, and up. If you fancy yourself a skilled driver, these hairpin curves will provide the perfect test. We had read an account of locals from the old days whose vehicles didn't possess the power to climb Sitgreaves Pass in forward gears — so they became experts at making the trip in reverse gear. As I peered down into the canyon, I couldn't imagine a more gruesome experience. Then we entered Ed's Camp, a place known for odd collectibles, but we had no room to stash trinkets. Amazing how you can fill the inside of a car.

Descending the pass, we passed by the ruins of Goldroad. Gold was discovered in the area in the 1860s by John Moss, and later silver ore was uncovered. The

(OPPOSITE PAGE) *Historic Route 66, marked by an Arizona Parkways, Historic and Scenic Roads sign, approaches the Black Mountains.*
(ABOVE, RIGHT) *A cluster of yuccas grows in the Black Mountains near the Sacramento Valley.*
(ABOVE) *Old Route 66 switchbacks through the Black Mountains en route to Oatman from Kingman.*

town's riches and existence ended abruptly when these veins gave out around 1907, and the town's owner razed the place in 1949 to avoid the taxes. So much for historical preservation. Now the ruins blend quite well into the surroundings, but if you look hard you'll find crumbling, weathered stones still stacked on top of each other. All around were roofless buildings and remnants of walls, concrete water tanks, miscellaneous mining equipment — and mine shafts, so be careful if you walk around.

If you make it this far, you can't help but notice the odd rocks lying about everywhere. Black on top, white on the bottom, they are volcanic remnants from the Black Mountains' active era, possibly debris left over from the same eruptions that created Peach Springs tuff near Kingman. Bob Yost of the Mohave Museum of History and Art in Kingman said "desert varnishing" causes the rocks to blacken on top. The sun leaches the chemicals right out of them. It's kind of a sunburn for rocks.

The next stop, Oatman, about five miles farther along the road, was the treat of the trip. We had to slow to a crawl as we entered town. Tourists, locals dressed like cowboys, and at least 20 burros mingled in a great hodge-podge in the middle of the street and along the sidewalks. The burros canvass the crowd for handouts, willing to accept anything, but signs posted all around request: carrots only, please! After we parked we immediately were hit up by friendly burros. But we were carrotless, so they trailed us all the way to the store, where we bought some.

We had wandered up the street a short way when a local cowboy picked up a mike and announced one of the weekend gunfights was about to begin. Mock gunfights happen regularly on weekends, and after the performance hats are passed around to collect donations for local charities. Afterward, donations were plentiful and I snapped a picture as one of the gunfighters made Chuck "stick-em up!"

Seeing the old jail is worth the dollar donation. Outside it, I had my picture taken on the old hangman's platform (I made sure and held the noose). There's an old wooden casket, and if you have a flash you can get great shots in the old cells.

Several local businesses display goods for sale, including shirts from the fire department. There are arts, crafts and critters of every kind on display. I gave the guys with the rattlesnake displays a wide berth. I'm sure the stealthy serpents were dead, but one can never be too sure.

We poked about town for a couple of hours, and still didn't feel ready to leave. There are some really neat shops

(LEFT) *Cold drinks and food served in miners' ambience help Oatman attract travelers.*
(OPPOSITE PAGE, TOP)
*Historic Route 66 runs through the old mining town of Oatman, now a tourist destination.*
(OPPOSITE PAGE, BOTTOM)
*Burros roam Oatman in search of handouts from tourists. Carrots are the preferred food.*

selling trinkets and merchandise of every kind. I fell in love with one shopkeeper's display of Confederate money. We also got a glimpse of an old mine (by peeking in — it was boarded up), and crept into the tiny one-room dwelling next to it (again carefully watching for snakes).

Then we toured the Oatman Hotel, a two-story adobe structure built in the 1920s. In 1939, according to a story told here, Clark Gable and Carole Lombard stayed at the hotel after being married in Kingman.

Later, we headed into one of the two restaurants in town. Both offer entertainment and good food.

Tourists and locals mix comfortably, and outsiders gain a keen appreciation for the staunch independence of the hometown folks. We enjoyed some of the coldest beer ever as we sat at a bar next to a cowboy who had lived in Oatman "forever." People came and went, leaving their money on the bar if they had a drink and a quarter if they used the phone. Everybody's on the honor system.

As Chuck and I left Oatman, my favorite little burro, a pinto colt, seemed to be saying good-bye as he watched me go.

From Oatman, it's about 20 paved miles to Golden Shores and a few more miles to Topock, both on the Colorado River. At Topock you'll see the arch bridge that once carried Route 66 traffic across the river. Or you can take the road west at the Y junction in Oatman, rather than the one south to Golden Shores. The road west takes you in 12 miles to State Route 95. From there, turn right for a quick trip to Bullhead City or left to return to I-40 at either Topock or Needles, California. ☙

## When You Go

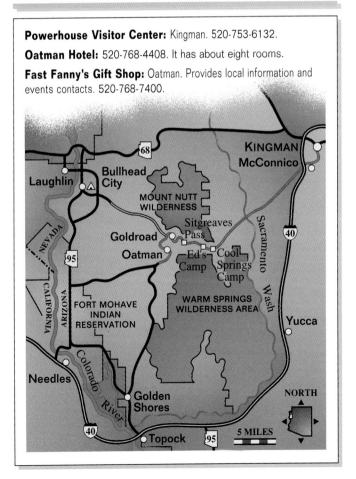

**Powerhouse Visitor Center:** Kingman. 520-753-6132.

**Oatman Hotel:** 520-768-4408. It has about eight rooms.

**Fast Fanny's Gift Shop:** Oatman. Provides local information and events contacts. 520-768-7400.

# Joshua Forest Scenic Parkway

**Photographs by Jack Dykinga**

**Name:** Joshua Forest Scenic Parkway.

**Route:** U.S. Route 93, between Wikieup and Wickenburg.

**Mileage:** 128 miles, Kingman to Wickenburg. (The scenic road covers 54 miles from Wikieup to just northwest of Wickenburg.)

**Time to allow:** Five to six hours.

**Elevation:** 3,300 feet at Kingman; 2,000 feet at Wikieup; 2,100 feet at Wickenburg.

**Overview:** Oftentimes, the attractions of this drive are overlooked by people in a hurry. Besides the Joshua tree, a giant member of the lily family, you'll pass through a landscape framed by a variety of mountains and graced by plants, wildlife, and history.

Joshua Forest Scenic Parkway covers much of the highway between Wickenburg and Wikieup, the route that many Arizonans with gambling fever take to the casinos of Laughlin and Las Vegas, Nevada. So intent are they upon reaching these slot-machine meccas that they never notice the beauty they pass through on their way. Or, perhaps they are making the trip in the summer, as I always had. There is precious little to appreciate when the sun makes you feel like a chicken roasting under a heat lamp.

While exploring this route, I must have exclaimed to myself 20 times, "All this is out there?" Each time I had cruised this highway before, it was either a summer night and too black to see anything but the headlights, or a summer afternoon when I was watching my skin burn and trying to get unstuck from my sister's vinyl seat.

This trip, however, we got lucky. It was late August, but monsoon season had arrived, and up at the northern end of the route, where we started, it was quite cool. The exit to U.S. Route 93 is about 20 miles east of Kingman off Interstate 40. There aren't many services once you turn off, so gas up before making the trip.

The Joshua Forest Scenic Parkway begins in Wikieup and covers just over 53 miles southeast to Wickenburg, following a path taken by Lt. Amiel Whipple in the 1850s as he surveyed a possible railroad route to the Pacific Coast. In Wikieup, we stopped at the Wikieup Trading Post, known for its fried rattlesnake (in season). The sign at the door reminds you to turn off your headlights, which are required, night and day, along most of this route.

Outside again, the Aquarius Mountains east of the parkway and the Hualapai Mountains to the west contrasted sharply against the silvery sky. Wikieup sits in the Big Sandy River flood plain, framed by the two mountain ranges. The vegetation includes stunning cottonwoods, their green color now standing out remarkably against the gray-green of the other desert shrubbery. The scene was a muted-color desert against a gray and white backdrop.

Just outside town, we noticed the steep, light green bluffs where the Big Sandy River has cut through sediments deposited there millions of years ago. Plant life is abundant along the parkway, and we found ocotillos;

*(OPPOSITE PAGE) The Joshua Forest extends for about 17 miles along U.S. Route 93. (ABOVE) Teddy bear cholla stands near the Big Sandy River drainage.*

saguaro and cholla cactuses; paloverde, mesquite, cottonwood, and sycamore trees; several varieties of wildflowers; and, of course, the Joshua trees.

The Joshua tree "forest" extends for about 17 miles and is one of three in the state. Named by Mormon settlers after the biblical Joshua with his arms raised in prayer, this tree-like yucca is a giant member of the lily family and may grow up to 30 feet tall. Joshua trees must depend on the pronuba moth to pollinate its flowers at night during March and April. Ancient Indians used the fruit for food and dyes, the fibrous leaves for basket making, and the stems for soap. Although they don't have growth rings, Joshua trees grow about an inch a year, some living to be more than 100 years old.

Moving southeast along the parkway, we soon passed over Burro Creek Bridge. At the bridge's scenic overlook we peered down into the canyon and found Burro Creek. Down the road three deer raced through the grass, leaping alongside us — did they really laugh at us for a moment? — before turning to dash off. Stunned momentarily, we watched their white tails vanish quickly toward Burro Creek Campground. We had never seen such a sight.

The campground's turnoff is just one mile south of the bridge, and then the drive in is about a mile and a half on a paved road. The Bureau of Land Management runs the campground, which includes picnic facilities, running water and flush toilets, an interpretive cactus garden, and

easy walking trails down to Burro Creek. Rockhounding, bird-watching, and hiking are all possibilities. There is a fee if you want to camp there.

Although there are no settlements between Wikieup and Wickenburg, there is one little sign of civilization around Milepost 148. Coming up over the hill, we saw a gravel parking area with a couple of small, frame buildings. This roadside stop is called Nothing and claims to have a population of four. More importantly, it has a gas pump, some mechanic services, and a bathroom.

The elevation had climbed somewhat and soon the road rolled smoothly along, winding through the cuts made in the various mountains and mesas. We could peek down at surrounding canyons and up at the odd granite knobs perched on some of the mountaintops. As we drove past clusters and heaps of rounded granite boulders, it began to rain. Rolling up my window, I decided the term "boulder field" was appropriate.

Any two-lane highway can seem narrow after six-lane freeways, but I noticed that often throughout the drive the road had absolutely no shoulder on either side, sometimes because of confining rock walls or steep drops. As we swooped around blind curves, I hoped we wouldn't meet a car drifting out of its lane because there was no place

(ABOVE) *The walls and trees — cottonwoods and willows — of Burro Creek Canyon reflect in Burro Creek.*
(LEFT) *Soaptree yucca flowers amid granite boulders along the Joshua Forest Scenic Parkway.*

(LEFT) *The Wickenburg Chamber of Commerce operates from a restored Santa Fe Railroad station on Frontier Street, not far from the Hassayampa River.*

for us to swerve. Some rather somber caution signs and multiple roadside crosses (22 before I lost count) told me that my concerns weren't groundless.

We passed the turn-off (State Route 71) leading to Congress and Yarnell, the latter definitely worth a visit if you have the time. My good friend and former schoolmate lives in Yarnell, and I make the trek up to visit her at least once a month. It's an hour and a half from Phoenix, but it might as well be a world away. It took me a few visits to accustom myself to the easy-going way of life that exists there. No one locks car doors or even the doors to their homes. We often walked the short distance to shop at the small grocery store, drop off mail, or visit the art gallery. But the hardware store is by far the most fun. So stop by if you can. The locals love visitors — only people who threaten to move there raise locals' hackles.

Wickenburg rests a short distance after the end of the route, and has plenty of its own charm. It's a ranching community, and trucks everywhere bear various ranch names on the doors. Horses and cattle graze alongside the road in fenced pastures in front of friendly-looking houses and barns. Everything has a quiet, hometown quality. Schools and shopping centers mix nicely with art galleries and a visitors center. The main street is packed with restaurants, motels and theaters, plus fast-food and quick-stop conveniences. Quite a change, in some respects, from what Wickenburg used to be like, I mused.

You see, Wickenburg wasn't always a peaceful little community. Named for Henry Wickenburg, it was once populated with hardened miners interested in finding riches. They didn't have time to build any facilities, not even a jail. Those who disobeyed the law were simply chained to the Jail Tree in the center of town until they served their time or sobered up, depending upon their offense. As we rounded the corner where U.S. 93 and U.S. 60 meet, I glanced behind the Circle K store at the huge tree still standing there, and smiled as I imagined the town rowdies in chains under its branches.

## When You Go

**Wickenburg Chamber of Commerce:** Restored Santa Fe Railroad station on Frontier Street along the tracks. From U.S. 93, turn west (right) on U.S. 60 and go a block or so to Frontier Street. Maps, pamphlets, lists of historic walking tours. 520-684-5479 or 800-942-5242. *www.wickenburgchamber.com*

**Desert Caballeros Western Museum:** Collections of ancient and modern crafts, rock and mineral specimens. Call for times and admission. 21 N. Frontier St. 520-684-2272/7075.

**Shrine of St. Joseph at Yarnell:** Twenty-five miles north of Wickenburg. At Congress exit, continue east on U.S. 89 to Yarnell. Restaurants, lodging in town. At center of town, a sign indicates the way to St. Joseph's Shrine. Statues depict the stations of the cross, and giant granite boulders add to the beauty of the spot. Small gift shop. Free admission.

**Hassayampa River Preserve (Nature Conservancy):** Teems with birds, other wildlife, and lush vegetation common to streamside areas. Nature walks, visitor center. Donations requested. Three miles south of Wickenburg on U.S. 60. 520-684-2772.

**Wickenburg annual events:** Gold Rush Days/Rodeo, second full weekend in February. Fiesta Septiembre, first Saturday in September. Celebrate Wickenburg's Hispanic heritage. Blue Grass Festival, second full weekend in November. Cowboy Poetry Gathering, first weekend in December. Contact chamber of commerce for details.

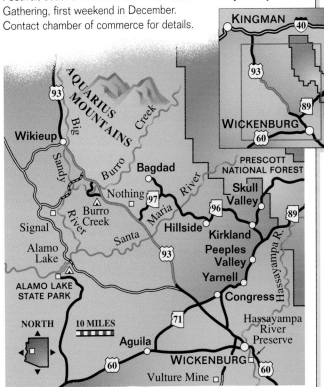

# Index

*Bold type indicates photograph.*

(PRECEDING PANEL, PAGES 108-109)
*The rolling grasslands near Sonoita have catered to cattle ranching since the 1800s.* RANDY A. PRENTICE
(OPPOSITE PAGE) *Cooley Lake on the Fort Apache Indian Reservation ripples by a stand of ponderosa pine trees.* JERRY JACKA
(ABOVE) *The early days — this sign once marked the highway that in 1984 received Arizona's first scenic road designation.* BOB & SUZANNE CLEMENZ

# Index

*Bold type indicates photograph.*

(LEFT) *Today Arizona's Parkways, Historic and Scenic Roads program marks roads with an updated variation of this logo.* JERRY SIEVE (OPPOSITE PAGE) *This decertified stretch of Route 66 near Ashfork Hill now is used mostly by bicyclists.* DAVID ELMS JR.